TALKING TO THE   REPTILIANS

A REPORT FROM BRAZIL

by

CHICO PENTEADO
(KRAAKAR   SHEM)

2010

Penteado,Chico Talking to the Reptilians-A Report from Brazil

2010, ISBN 978-0-557-57653-1

Contact the author: chicopenteado@hotmail.com

INDEX

INTRODUCTION

PART1-THE KRAAKAR CASE:

EARLY VIGILS

MS.DIVA'S HOUSE

MY FIRST ABDUCTION

PARANORMAL ACTIVITY

THE STRANGER AT THE BUS STATION

TRYING TO UNDERSTAND THE EXPEREINCES

I AM KRAAKAR

PAST LIFE MEMORIES

WHY SO MUCH AVERSION TO REPTILIANS?

MENTAL CONTACT IS LESS DISTURBING THAN PHYSICAL ABDUCTION

PART 2-OTHER REPORTS

OTHER PEOPLE AND THEIR REPORTS

ROMULO'S REPORT:A PSYCHIC

MR. MANGA:PURE IN THE HEART

HANS' CASE:"NORDICS" AREN´T ALWAYS THAT NICE

ICARUS'S CASE: INCUBUS SUCUBUS?

JACOB'S CASE:"BECAUSE YOU ARE VERY SPECIAL"

KARREL'S CASE:FERTILITY

HEBE,MY MOTHER

ABOUT THE AUTHOR

BIBLIOGRAPHY

IMPORTANT SITES

INTRODUCTION

Sooner or later, you will find what you are looking for. This has always been my motto. I have never paid attention to people who tried to scare me by telling eerie stories involving aliens. People are too afraid of ufo observation vigils, they no longer go out at night in isolated places, and they are no longer willing to observe skies and fields, looking for unusual flying phenomena. Watching the skies seems to be an easy task, but nowhere could I find a bunch of people who could be possibly interested in that. Over the years, I found many ufo research groups who were basically readers and talkers, discussing topics from important authors or watching videos related to that topic. Eventually, these groups investigate abduction cases that happened to somebody else. Most groups do not go to the middle of nowhere for a ufo observation vigil, at least not here in Brazil. They do not believe that someone might summon this phenomenon upon oneself. They tend to think UFO abduction as a totally casual phenomenon, something that happens by accident, like observing a meteor or a comet, something that happens to a few people somewhere. I have never accepted that.

Besides, the American ufo scene nowadays tends to be pessimistic, based on horrifying stories of gray aliens who are taking people in the thousands and forcing them to participate in a most unpleasant alien-human hybridization program.Aliens whose intentions are selfish and useless to mankind as a whole. That is the predominant view nowadays. These gray aliens would probably be producing a slave race, or maybe trying to save their own decadent genes, or anything else that does no good to us.

Therefore, UFO observation vigils are no longer fashionable. People used to gather in remote places at night, back in the 50's,60's and 70's,just gazing at the night skies, hoping to see something unusual, but the ufo research scene is no longer so. Many see alien contact as a flirt with insanity and pain, an encounter with malevolent aliens. As a matter of fact, people began to avoid lingering in dark rural areas at night.And that was because they knew about the existence of aliens and the terrible things they do to both humans and animals. This is the new phase of ufo research, the "age of the fear of extraterrials", the age we are living today.

Nevertheless, one day I finally found a group of lunatics like myself who is still doing such vigils. People never stop asking me: "-Don't you know what happens to the ones who are taken? How dare you? Are you out of your mind?"The same people who reads and believes in UFOs and aliens said such things to me. They even told me I would end up being eaten by aliens someday. But I tell you what: nobody in my group so far has ever died because of ufo observation vigils or for being abducted by a real nasty alien.

Besides, most UFO vigils are absolutely boring. It is very frustrating when nothing happens. The leader of the ufo research group I belong to, I will call her "Isis" (she can not be identified for many reasons), compares an uneventful vigil to an unsuccessful fishing. It is just as boring, and she calls it "bait washing day", lengthy vigil nights for nothing. Most people expect immediate success. They have heard of George Adamski, or maybe they have seen "Close Encounters of the Third Kind" by Spielberg, and they hope to find about the same. But as it does not usually happen this way, most people will give up soon.

People who still practice UFO vigils tend to become superstitious just like fishermen. Both activities depend a lot on luck. I tried almost everything to improve my chances. I prayed, I bought amulets, crystals, witchcraft. Nothing really worked. But I still believe that a proper mental state makes a big difference. Therefore I do not have sex before a ufo vigil. I do not drink alcoholic beverages before a vigil. Besides, I have been a vegetarian for over 25 years. Chanting mantras seemed to help getting concentration. Mystic symbols, on the other hand, did not make any difference. Someone once gave me a symbol created by Samael Aum Weor(< http://www.gnosisonline.org>).This friend of mine claimed it would attract alien contact, and we printed it really huge, and placed it right in the middle of the ufo vigil spot. But it never worked, at least not for me.

 But I am sure that a good rapport among the group members does make a difference. Despite of our individual differences, we must get along well, at least during the vigil. Each and every one of us is different in terms of taste, gender, social class, religion, political tendencies, sexual preference, and ethnicity. There will always be someone who does, or says, or believes in something we dislike. I am sure that aliens observe our internal relationships, the way we deal with one another. They are probably not interested in a broken group with a lot of internal aversions. So, we must learn how to get along better, at least during those vigil hours. It is a peace making exercise. And it is incredibly hard, since we must stay together for hours, doing nothing, right in the middle of nowhere.The perfect place for an argument.

It is also mandatory that all group members be ready for the experience. Whenever there is a new member, this person tends to reduce our chances a little. It is often so that people want to participate out of sheer curiosity. Sometimes we do not notice that our new guest has a tone of mockery concerning what we are doing there, or that his or her intentions are not serious.But believe me, aliens do sense that. They are telepathic and they know exactly what is going on, there is no lying possible to them. Or if someone comes along with a new girlfriend or a relative who is not really interested, this makes the whole difference. So I suggest we select the ones who are allowed to participate in a UFO vigil, otherwise it will be a total waste of time. Moreover, participants should try to talk about UFOs or spirituality related topics as much as possible, in order to create the right atmosphere.Otherwise they had better remain in silence.

But there are some who are lucky right from the beginning. They get there only once and they end up seeing something really great. Some years ago we received a group of teenagers who had been to a UFO vigil for the very first time, and as we got there, there were two bright white lights waiting for us at the end of the road. They remained there for some time and then left without a sound or a trace. It seems like aliens want to foster awareness among the youth. But unfortunately, none of these three has ever come back for more.

This also happens to some die-hard skeptics who make fun of ufo believers. A girl called Katia used to say she did not really believed in my stories. Once I took her to the exact place where I usually do my vigils, deep in the night. As soon as we got there, a huge ball of white fire fell down some 5 meters far from where we were. It fell down vertically and it faded away silently some 2 feet from the ground, without any explosion whatsoever. We left some time after, and she never bothered me again. The same thing happened to a Frenchman, who claimed to be a "rational" person. I guess he meant I was not. He stayed over in the country house where I usually stay after my vigils. But on that specific weekend I was obliged to stay in Sao Paulo.I was having dinner in a mall, and suddenly I received a call from this Frenchman. He sounded scared and he asked: "Those blue lights flying above me,do you think will they take me away or not?" This one too, he never messed with me again.That is why I tell you not to worry about the skeptics, no need to prove them anything. If aliens decide to do so, they will do it themselves. And oftentimes, even though they did see a UFO, those skeptics insist on denying what they have seen.

This book deals essentially with the three most commonly reported aliens species, which is, the grays, the humanoids (mainly the "Nordics") and the reptilians. Authors such as David Jacobs and Budd Hopkins have already shown everything there is about the grays and their possible origin as from Zeta Reticuli, as well as their appearance and behavior. Witnesses rarely talk positively about them. The Brazilian ufo researcher Marcos Antonio Petit is an exception, since he claimed in his book that a gray alien saved his life in a car accident by preventing him from falling off a cliff.("Ufos, Espiritualidade e Reencarnação" ,Ed do Conhecimento, 1ª Ed.2004). In his book "the

Keepers", the American contactee Jim Sparks is also an exception, as he moves from a relationship of fear towards the gray aliens to another of understanding and learning. (Sparks, Jim –The Keepers, Wild Flower Press, 2006).

Most authors tend to present the grays as hostile, a kidnapper who performs hybridization experiments with humans and that is all. And this would be of no advantage to mankind at all. But I believe it is not that simple.

Human-looking or more specifically Nordic aliens, on the other hand, are much more welcome, since they are beautiful to our eyes and apparently more "human". Spiritualistic UFO societies such as the former Rama group (nowadays called Sunesis project) try a contact with those, especially Captain Ashtar Sheran or Metaron, and they trust them completely. They barely ever think of a non-Confederate Nordic alien whose intentions would be bad. They think they are good, period.

Reptilians, as the name says, seem to have evolved from some kind of reptile instead of a mammal, and they are said to originate from Orion, more specifically the Orion belt, the stars Alnitak, Alnilam and Mintaka respectively(those names are the traditional ones in Arabic).The origin of such information is questionable though it is widespread. These beings are always considered as having a very evil nature and they were more recently associated to the illuminati society and their allegedly evil deeds. Many authors, especially David Icke devoted their careers to demonstrate how evil they are as well as their wicked connections to the most powerful men on Earth. Such powerful human families would descend upon the reptilians themselves and they would be willing to do just anything to retain their power. Or at least they would have an agreement with those reptilian beings, whatever that means. For authors such as David Icke, reptilians only care about domination or exploitation, and they would have actually led mankind to the miserable situation it is in today. There seems to be a clear association between reptilians and Satan in Icke's works.

Few people would admit publicly to have been in contact with reptilians, especially if that contact was pleasant or positive. Once again Jim Sparks' book "The Keepers" appears as an exception, as he describes the reptilians behind the grays who took him at first. Later in his book, those reptilians meet him in an abandoned amusement park at night, initially disguised as humanoids. ("The Keepers" pages 167 to 174, Wild Flower Press, 2006) Jim somehow suspected they were not really human-looking beings, and in a certain moment requested that they show their real face to him. They hesitated for a while, but finally they agreed to do so. After that they talked for a long time, and those reptilians admitted having contact with human rulers. They said those human governments had promised to disclose the alien contact reality once and for all, though gradually, but this has never really happened since those men in power would try to maintain their condition no matter what it takes. Therefore, the reptilian group suggested an amnesty to those politicians, so that they would not be smashed by an infuriated human mob.

Jim considered the reptilians "neither good nor evil, just different". He felt they would not destroy or take over planet Earth, although they intend to take some natural resources whenever necessary. They did not deny that.

American jazz singer Pamela Stonebrooke, also known as "The intergalactic Diva" spoke publicly about her relationship with a reptilian being who visited her at night. At first she thought he would be some Greek god, but later she realized it was a strong, scaly reptilian alien. Nevertheless she felt intense pleasure in his presence, a familiar presence to her. The entity said: "-Don´t worry, we´ve known each other for so long, we love each other."And she finally understood that shape shifting is a normal thing for alien beings (of all kinds, I would add).This occurred in 1998, although she had been having alien contacts since 1994. As usual, her early experiences were with the grays, who escorted her to some sort of nursery with a lot of female hybrid alien babies. They all called her "mom". She found that extremely disturbing, and she became insomniac for over a year. And by admitting her unusual relationship, she suffered a lot of opposition and eventually lost her job. Nevertheless, she still stands up bravely for her case in interviews or in her own site< www.intergalacticdiva.com> .

The reports I am about to present are a combination of different kinds of experiences:

1-Actual abduction experiences, physical experiences as they are felt in the "real" material world we live in.

2-Astral projection experiences, lucid dreams, meditative states, near-sleep states, "spiritual states of mind."These are special opportunities to access our deeper minds and our connections with extraterrials or whatever beings who exist in other dimensions. These are fundamental for understanding our alien contacts, since the actual gray alien abduction contains little or no dialogue and teachings. Since aliens can erase our memories partially or completely, the reminiscent memory tends to look like a dream. One must not ignore this source of information simply by considering it non-scientific.

3-Channeling experiences, telepathic experiences. Contactees tend to receive psychic messages from time to time. These are just like computer downloads of insight, even if that person is not usually a very bright-minded one. In these moments it is obvious there is something different going on, as someone who is perfectly ordinary begins talking like a philosopher or a scientist totally out of the blue. It is evident that it is some sort of external influence, a glimpse of ingeniosity. Sometimes, the bearer of such messages may choose when, where and if he or she would convey the massage.But at times, he or she is forced to do so. This individual will start speaking or writing immediately, no matter what he/she is doing, and will not rest until it is finished. But most of the times, telepathic messages are more subtle though they are repeatedly echoing in the contactee´s mind.

PART 1-THE KRAAKAR CASE

MY EARLY VIGILS

I am the author of this book, as well as the witness of the story I am about to tell. I am an ordinary man, a middle class Brazilian. I work as an English language teacher in a language institute, a middle aged person. I was born in the huge and rather unattractive city of Sao Paulo and I spent most of my life there. I also spent some years in the Netherlands, but, apart from that, I led a boring life which is not worth talking about. I have always been interested in philosophy, arts, religions, especially Buddhism and Afro-Brazilian cults, spiritualism in general and environmentalism. Since I was a child, I have always been kind of strange, I did not socialize much, and if I tried to do so, it was always a disaster. On the other hand,I would say I was a talented student of languages and history. I grew up in the 1970's, right in the middle of the disco music days and under a fierce military dictatorship that ruled the country back then.

In those days, incredible as it may seem, there were more and better documentaries and TV shows talking about UFO research or occultism than nowadays. I have a feeling there is a much stronger censorship in Brazilian TV today than back in the old days of military dictatorship. A hidden kind of censorship and I do not really understand who is behind that. I used to dream of living the experiences that some people claimed to have had, all those UFOs and alien encounters.I never understood why this happened to someone who was not at all interested, and it did not happen to me. Back then, people used to have a more positive view of aliens, they were not yet convinced that alien contact was all about scary grays abducting people in a most unpleasant biological experiment. They accepted the alien presence as a totally unsolved mystery, and in my humble opinion, this is still the case. People nowadays talk as if they already knew it all, as if the alien agenda had already been revealed. How pretentious!

I attended many UFO congresses and lectures, but I never got to know a real good UFO research group where I could participate and go together to a UFO vigil on a regular basis. I had heard of the General Uchoa's incredible experiences afield, his mysterious visions and channelings, but there was nobody like him near me. Finally I met a famous research in those days called Osni Schwarz in one of those congresses, but unfortunately he passed away a few months later. I was totally out of luck. Therefore, I wasted 37 years of my life without learning much about this topic, until I started dating someone who lived in the countryside in 2002. Until that moment, I had always been profoundly urban, Sao Paulo has a population of over 18 million people, you will not see any natural landscape if you drive through it for hours. The first time I heard a cow mooing, I ran! But I began visiting the middle sized town of Piracicaba regularly, and there were many tiny towns around it, and those were surrounded by mountains and farms. In one of those trips, I got to know a woman, I will call her "Isis", because she lives in a very small town and she could get in trouble there. She managed to organize a UFO vigil group, and most of these people were abductees and contactees themselves. Isis was a very experienced researcher, she knew everything about UFOs, both in Brazil and abroad, and she was a contactee herself. Back in the 90's, she had had her own experiences, but I promised not to tell, because she might be willing to write a book of her own someday. I was really lucky this time. I accepted her invitation to participate immediately. Isis is a retired woman.She is an animal protector who runs a shelter with over 60 abandoned dogs nowadays in a country where nobody helps her at all.

In one of those visits to Piracicaba, I was on the road at around 4p.m. in a sunny day when I saw a huge cigar-shaped UFO It was a silver one, spinning like a record, hovering above the tall trees. I saw there was a bus on the other side of the road, the bus was broken and people were outside pointing at it. That was my very first experience, and I knew I was doing the right thing, and that was the ultimate confirmation. After some 30 seconds, the object shrank in itself, it is hard to explain, it was like the image of an old TV set being turned off.

I think of that as "the wake up call'. By talking to many contactees, it became clear to me that most of them had seen UFOs prior to their actual contact experience. It is just like the Bible says: "-For many are invited, but few are chosen.'(Matthew 22; 14).The same goes for alien contact. So many people have seen UFOs, but not many are touched in their hearts by it.

For many people, the fact that they saw an UFO has little or no effect on their lives.They do not go for vigils and the end up forgetting it sooner or later. They tend to see it as a purely casual thing. That is a pity. They are not aware of how selective these beings are, they do not know they were chosen. They do not know that aliens can move around in invisibility, so that they can be seen only **when** and **if** they feel like.

So off I went to my first UFO vigil with Isis and her group. Some group members go, others remain, that depends on how deep is their connection to the phenomenon. I participated in one, two, ten, a hundred, two hundred vigils or more, in different locations near Botucatu hills, but we usually do it in a valley called Novo Horizonte ("The New Horizon", a very suggestive name, by the way...), in the outskirts of a small town called Charqueada, some 160 miles far from Sao Paulo, the capital city of the state. Although it is a beautiful place, it is not considered particularly attractive to tourists, and local farmers grow sugar cane or raise cattle. As usual for Brazil, there are plenty of untouched areas, and I hope it stays that way. The weather is subtropical and it can be very cold in Southern hemisphere wintertime, say, June and July, with temperatures below the freezing point at night. Southern Brazil is quite different from the rest of the country, it is a cool region occupied mainly by people of Italian, Polish, German or even Japanese origin who immigrated in the early years of the 20th century.

We did not choose a place high up in the hills ,we preferred a valley location where we could see the strange lights that move around the pasture. We heard stories from the farmers who claimed that this area called "Novo Horizonte"was haunted. They did not consider those lights as UFOs.Instead they would call them "mãe-do-ouro", 'mother-of-gold", a bright, moving, intelligent light that they believe is a spirit who guards goldmines, a Brazilian superstition. It is no use calling them UFOs among the very simple people who live in rural areas. You should say "mãe-do-ouro", instead, and they will tell you a million stories about that.

The most important factor for choosing a location for a UFO vigil is finding a place as secluded from the human presence as possible. No houses or towns in sight, not too many cars passing by, no residential areas. Most of the times we do it in small groups of two to five people, no more, otherwise it may not work. If the group is too big, we will split in different areas. We also believe that going repeatedly to the same place and in the same day, which is on Saturdays basically, would create a routine that both we and the aliens alike would relate to. Sometimes I dare to do it all alone, those vigils are the best, how scary they are!

As I said ,oftentimes nothing happens, but eventually the aliens play tricks on us, they show something apparently normal which is in fact one of their devices. Once, we saw a little red light that could be a normal plane, moving in a regular speed and in a straight line, nothing much really.

Suddenly that thing fell down vertically over the hill, with absolutely NO sound or explosion whatsoever. The lesson they teach here is how good they are at disguising themselves.

There are also more and less intensive UFO activity periods, the so called "waves'. I think 2005 was the best wave of all for us. A memorable year where I felt like I was in a close connection with them, in constant communication, sensing when they were around and when they were not. The following years were somewhat less intensive, and the present year 2010 has been unusually weak. That scares me.It makes me think this planet is about to be shaken and they know that, therefore they would be leaving ahead of time. I hope I am wrong about that.

It was a Saturday night in August, 2005, I am not sure which one exactly, I was not feeling well that day, and I had a moderate flu. I had a headache; my body was aching all over. Nevertheless, I felt a strong urge to travel since I knew there was going to be a vigil in Sao Pedro, a small town near Piracicaba, yet I was feeling some strange euphoria that could overcome the pain and I decided to go anyway. Marcelo offered me a ride to Sao Pedro, and, when I got there, I realized Isis was not feeling well, either. It seemed like everything that could go wrong, did.

As we got to that remote vigil place, I was looking at the

beautiful pasture after we parked in a small road next to a farm. We could see the city lights from a distance but there were no houses around. That road was on the top of those hills and we could se everything a little below us. Suddenly a bright yellowish light appeared from behind one of those hills, some 500 meters from where we were. It looked like a normal light at first; it was not odd at all. But it grew bigger and brighter and I was amazed that Isis had not noticed it. There were Just the two of us, and one of those telepathic commands told me:"-Take a picture now!"

That is most unusual, since they never really allow us to bring home any evidence or anything. So I did, and for my surprise I realized the bright light had some kind of human shape!(see pictures 1 and 2).Its background is pitch-dark, I did not use the flash for that picture, and it seemed like that thing was near the horizon line, a little above that. By zooming the image, which is pretty small originally, I could see a human-like being with seemed to be enclosed by some door or window, a being whose legs and arms seemed to be hidden behind the straight lines of that window. The whole background behind her was equally black. It is a blurred image and I can not distinguish any facial features, but I have the impression she had black hair.

It looks like a woman, a naked woman or a woman wearing a shinny, glowing, tight overall. I can easily distinguish female breasts and female hips in her, I think of it as a female. I also had an impression there was another being behind her, a darker, brownish one with a large oval head, more like a gray alien, but I am not at all sure of that. It is impossible to see more details than those I mentioned here.

Surprisingly, Isis seemed totally indifferent to it, and I felt like hiding my enthusiasm for some reason. The light faded soon, and I received another telepathic message. The voice said: "-I am Female Shem, your therapist, responsible for your case. Don´t tell her you have seen me yet" I do not usually lie to Isis, but I decided to obey. I was overjoyed although I was worried as well, I did not know how far this would go. That UFO vigil ended early, as we both were not feeling fine that day. Besides, nothing else happened.

This is by far the best gift they have ever given to me, I treasure this picture so much, I keep it next to the pictures of my dearest deceased relatives in my bedroom. A day to remember for sure. I also thought it was really funny how she wanted to be addressed as "Female Shem", which is not too polite for us Earthlings. We would probably call her "Doctor" or "Miss", or"Madam", but she preferred "Female" instead. An alien thing, their behavior will always amaze us. Do not expect to apply your logic to them. And now I know her name and I think about her before my vigils, I kind of connect mentally to her during my vigils. I have other pictures of UFOs and other weird things ,but they are quite mediocre in comparison, and definitely not as meaningful as this one. That is why I am showing it to you, and I will always confirm its authenticity no matter what people think or say.

Even though I tried to enhance brightness and contrast in Photoshop experiments later, nothing else appears in it that could clarify or explain that image a little. It is just the bright being against a dark background and that is all. This is quite frustrating, but there is nothing I can do about it. Later I also realized the word "Shem" means "Name" in Hebrew, such as in "Hashem" ("The Name"), one of the terms used to refer to God. But I am not a Jew and I did not hear about that until very recently. It is mere coincidence, I suppose.

However, whenever I feel that funny kind of euphoria, that means they are around. This happened again some years later. It was a boring Tuesday in Sao Paulo, a place where I do not expect to see a UFO and I was giving a class in an office building located at Indianopolis Avenue. The class would finish at 7 p.m., and some thirty minutes before the end of it I began to feel that strange kind of happiness. Up to that moment, I was feeling bored and empty inside, as I usually feel on Mondays and Tuesdays. But suddenly I felt invaded by a wave of pleasure and inner light, some kind of epiphany, almost.

When my job was over, I left the building and crossed the avenue. The bus system of Sao Paulo is awful, and I was expecting to wait for 45 minutes or more for my bus. It was a warm evening with a beautiful clear sky. That avenue is full of prostitutes, and two hookers were standing there waiting for a customer, chatting and laughing out loud near me.

A big shinny star appeared in the sky near the office tower and began to move around randomly, pretty much like a fly would. It was hovering above the building, it stood still for a minute then it got brighter and bigger until it became the size of a full moon. After that, it shrank back to a normal star size and disappeared. All that lasted one or two minutes. Meanwhile the two hookers kept on talking silly things, ignoring completely the fact that I was mesmerized by that sight. That is exactly why I laugh when some people say: "-There are no UFOs, I've never seen one!"If I hear that, I always reply: "-Well, how often do you look at the skies?"People are looking down or sideways most of the time. How could they possibly notice a UFO? Are they waiting for a UFO with a siren or a noisy bell? UFOs usually make no sound, and if you are not attentive, maybe you will never see one. And there might be one really close to you, much closer than you expect…Even when they travel to the countryside, most people keep on making noises and their occupations. Music, beer, barbecue, sports. Few people really enjoy nature and silence, at least in Brazil.

However, they expect to see a UFO someday. They hope it will fly low, right on their faces, otherwise they will not pay attention to some dim light up there in the sky. It does not work that way; unfortunately, aliens are very, very subtle.

The same situation happened some time later at the Ibirapuera Park, 6 p.m. in a summer evening. The place was crowded. People were jogging, playing soccer, flirting. Some stars appeared in the sky, but they were moving back and forth. Firstly I thought they were satellites, but those were performing angles and moving backwards. It was a silent, discreet, yet enthralling scene. And once again, I was the only one who noticed it. Nobody else stopped doing whatever they were doing to look up and check it out for a single second.

That joyful sensation came back again one night when I was returning back from work late. It was around 10 p.m. The bus finally arrived after another bitter waiting time of 30 minutes or more, as usual. I sat in the bus, exhausted. And suddenly I had that happy feeling again. We were passing by a dark square; there was nobody there that late. The voice said: "-Get off!", and so I did. There I was, all alone, in a dark empty square, in a dangerous city such as Sao Paulo.

It took no more than a couple of minutes before the "dancing stars" began their performance. They moved in crazy ways reassuring their extraordinary nature to me. They crossed each other's way; they moved back and forth, they performed acute angles. And then, they stopped and another bus passed, this time it did not take long. That too seemed like a miracle to me. I am truly thankful to them for such small gifts. That really makes my day.

Fig. 1-The bright human figure on the hill, 2005(enlarged image).The being identified herself as "Female Shem", São Pedro, Brazil. (Property of the author Chico Penteado)

Fig. 2- Female Shem, the picture in its original before enlargement.(Property of the author Chico Penteado)

Fig.3- Kraakar, by Kraakar. (Property of the author Chico Penteado)

Another funny thing about aliens is their curiosity towards our emotions. Any emotional outbursts tend to make the aliens come closer for a peek. Two of my UFO group members began to argue during a vigil once. They were almost shouting at each other, quite angrily. They sounded like they hated each other that night. At that very moment, a huge, cone shaped light in bright green passed slowly above us all, so silently. It hovered above the mountains for some seconds and went away after shrinking to the size of a small green star. Needless to say, the argument stopped immediately. Nothing else happened that day.

If you are experienced in UFO vigils, you know they usually do not allow taking pictures. It is all for eyes only. In the beginning, I invested heavily in cameras in a typically scientific UFO research fashion, but later I realized that was exactly what they did NOT want from me. We are not supposed to give away their secrets. If you have a special location for your encounters, this must remain secretive. At first I was looking for the ultimate piece of evidence, but later I learnt that they disappear as soon as we point a camera at them. And you will never trick them. There are good reasons for that: Firstly, we shall not attract curious people who can harm their well being and privacy, especially if we are close to their hidden bases. One must consider the fact that they are not really arriving from outer space, they might be coming from some hidden facility located in a nearby mountain, lake or sea. They excavate solid rock with their powerful tools and have access to places we could not reach. All of that is done so in order to keep their location inaccessible to us, because we are most undesirable neighbors. And too many pictures and evidence could help humans to track down their hiding places. That can not be.

Even if we knew where they stay while on Earth, we probably would not locate the entrance gate anyway, unless they invite us to go inside. They can easily delude our eyes with holograms. For instance, one of those nights Isis and I were coming back from a perfectly useless UFO vigil night. We took the usual road, and we knew it like the palm of our hands. All of a sudden, we realized we were in a different place, another road. It could be somewhere else in that region, but we had never been there before. The road we used to take had no detour, no alternatives. It was just a rough path of pounded earth. So, how could we possibly miss it? After a few minutes, Isis asked me if I had noticed something strange about the road, and I immediately said YES! I saw things that do not belong in the usual road, such as a white, American style fence which does not match the local farming styles, and houses we had never seen before. But once again, in the wink of an eye, we were back to the normal road again, totally out of the blue.

There are many possible interpretations for that. Firstly I thought of an abduction followed by the implantation of false memories. Therefore I called my hypnosis therapist, but we did not uncover any abduction detail apart from the strangeness of the road in itself. If something really serious and traumatic took place that night, its memories are strongly concealed under such false memories. No matter how hard we tried, nothing else came out.

Another important event is the so called "flying stork". It was a normal night, Isis and I were leaning on a farm fence when a semi-transparent, whitish object came from somewhere behind us both, flying low. It looked like a big bird-like machine. It was winged and it was kind of "potbellied", although it did not have anything like a head, just a long neck ending in a straight cut. It reminded me of a Concorde jet plane in miniature, some weird device, really. It was very aerodynamic in design, although it did not seem to be made of solid matter. Its consistency is hard to describe. It was a bit like egg white a few seconds after you drop it in a frying pan, just a thin membrane.

Nevertheless, the thing could interact with solid bodies. It hit Isis's right arm when it passed, and she felt it rubbing her arm very strongly. The next day, her right arm was swollen and bruised, although she did not feel much of an intense pain. We returned home that night some time after that with no further events.

Later that night, I went back to Ms. Diva´s house where I stayed over whenever I went to Sao Pedro. Ms. Diva was an old lady who is no longer among us. She had two daughters, namely Marcia and Maria who were gracious about inviting me to stay there. That house was perfect. It was quite removed from the downtown area, with a beautiful garden in the back, where I would go on with my vigil until very deep in the night. I did so whenever Isis felt tired and wanted to go home too early. And it was in that very location that I had the most amazing experiences, all alone. Everybody else went to bed, while I would remain out there in the dark. In that specific night when the "stork" showed up, I saw it over again, flying fast right above my head, some 30 feet above me.

 The following day we were both sick, with a strong nausea and some black diarrhea. Isis vomited. For that reason she interpreted that as an "attack", according to what American UFO researchers like David Jacobs or Budd Hopkins usually say about those beings ,describing them as hostile or, at least, indifferent to human beings. Obviously, that would be the ultimate evidence of that. But I had a different point of view. I understood that there could be another reason for that, as my psychic abilities blossomed after that event. I believe they altered my energetic body, my chakras.Many gurus in India, such as the Great Sai Baba are capable of doing this with a simple gesture, by using a specific Mudra.People who had this experience also claim they got sick afterwards. I suppose aliens do that too, in order to communicate more easily with us. They see us as "blind "or "disabled" by nature, because we do not have as much of psychic powers as they do, so they correct it artificially.

I had one more great experience with Isis. This one occurred in 2009,we were doing our usual vigil when we saw a bright yellowish light appear some 20 feet far from us on the ground, amongst the pasture grass. It looked pretty much like a normal car light, but it was in an impossible place, in direct contact with the soil. It began to move randomly, like a rat running in the field, running and stopping here and there. Then it climbed a small tree and it began to light up its branches, behaving as if it was displaying its abilities to us. We did not record that, because we knew it would stop the moment we turned the cameras on, so we decided to watch and enjoy this unique moment. After some minutes, it disappeared completely and it never came back.

Since Isis is a great researcher herself, I will not report all the amazing stories she told me over the years. She had other UFO research groups before and those had experienced a lot of things and investigated many cases. She said an extraterrial being told her once: "-You must do 90% of the hard work, we do the other 10%"(in order to get a contact).I would say she did more than that...she is restless when it comes to UFO research. Therefore, I hope she writes a book of her own anytime soon, which will be much better than mine!

MS. DIVA´S HOUSE

My dearest lady Diva is no longer among us. As per her invitation I have stayed over in her house for years, the same house nowadays occupied by her daughters Marcia and Maria and visited by Diva's youngest son Marcelo who is now in his forties. Marcelo works in a stationery store in Sao Paulo, and he often travels to the countryside where the rest of the family stays, so that I can ask him for a ride. This family lives some 150 miles from the capital city of Sao Paulo, and the house is spacious and there is a big garden where the backyard should be. Strangely enough, the backyard is in the front side of the house, and they cook outside in that front area, a very typical country habit in Brazil. In that "back garden" as I call it, there is a swimming pool and a large grill area and I sit there for hours, deep at night, just looking at the stars, waiting for something to arrive. Piracicaba region has one of the best skies for astronomical observation in Brazil. The night sky view over there is stunning. And a lot of events took place in that garden.

It was back in 2007, I saw a big ball of fire, the size of a soccer ball appearing in the sky some 20 feet above me and coming down slowly. It was tremendously scary, It looked like real fire and it seemed like it could burn me alive easily. In a given moment, that ball was near me, some three meters far from me. It behaved intelligently, it moved according to the outer wall contours of that house. Firstly the right wall, than the rear wall, then the left wall, and finally hovered above the house for a moment. It was very threatening, and it moved away, until it ended up above the hill behind the house and vanished. At first, I interpreted that as an invitation to walk up that hill, but that was a very hard thing to do. But I also felt as if they meant something like: '-You are watching us, and we are watching you." That is probably what they meant.

In other occasion, I saw a white ball of fire hit the roof of their house, just like a meteor would do, but with absolutely no harm to anything or anyone. The same happened to the hill behind the house, those balls of fire would collide against the solid rock causing no noise or damage whatsoever. Sometimes there were green and blue ones, and eventually they would cause a quick blackout. Of course I do not think those blackouts are just a coincidence. Some of those things are more oddly shaped, like a pill, or sometimes they come together like a pearl string. They also appear in purple, red or pink, sometimes slowing down or making angular movements. That is how they show they are more than just strange meteors. People in the countryside see so many things like that they no longer care about them. These people keep doing their things without paying them any attention. That is incredible to me. I go wild when I see a good ball of light like that. I was born in a big city with permanently foggy skies and this is still totally new to me.

Those balls of light interact with humans, sometimes following them in a kind of hot pursuit, especially when someone drives a car in deserted roads deep in the night. This is constantly reported by local people. They also send out flashes of a light similar to the one of a human camera, and these flashes have effects on people. The father of a friend of mine who lives in Sao Pedro had been submitted to an eye surgery that went wrong. He was about to go blind in his left eye. One of the lights came down to his backyard and shone a flash light upon him and the next day he was healed.

I have always suspected there was something special in that old lady Diva. She had always been obsessed by locking doors and closing windows, she was always scared of invaders. As a young woman, she had worked for a wealthy family in Sao Paulo as a governess. She was physically strong and somewhat authoritarian, also a perfectionist. By the time she passed away she was 81 years old although she smoked two packs of cigarettes a day. She used to say strangers were entering the house all the time and she was also afraid of those balls of light she had seen so many times. Family members thought she was demented or paranoid, but I believed her, and I knew how awful is to say those things where no one believes us. I knew she was a psychic and possibly a contactee. Only her youngest son Marcelo agreed with me.

It seemed that everyone there was involved in it one way or another. Marcelo, when he was a kid, had seen a tiny

UFO coming out from behind a TV set. There was a tiny glass dome on the top of it. He could see a gray alien in miniature inside that dome, just a few inches tall, and it looked like a toy. Completely scared, he ran to his mother.

At first I thought that case was too weird even for me. Surprisingly enough I heard the same thing from another boy, I will call him "F.S', and they did not know each other. F.S used to live in Rio de Janeiro when he was 6 or 7 years old and his mother left his bedroom window wide open in one of those very hot nights. She went to bed and a small UFO entered through the window, with a tiny gray alien inside as well. The little creature did not look at the kid. It was just flying around the room, as if it was observing the objects in it. F.S. darted out of the room and called his mother who took him in her own bedroom. She told him to calm down. Then she told him that he had seen some strange butterfly. And what a butterfly, I would say!

A few days after this weird encounter, Marcelo developed a strange disease in his legs. He was about 8 years old back then. It looked like some kind of smallpox, infectious, smelly and dark, a very disgusting thing. Other kids at school were so disgusted that he was obliged to quit school for a year. They disappeared by themselves, although no doctor managed to find out what it was. Another curious fact is that Marcelo has never gotten a flu or a cold ever since.

Marcelo's sister Marcia lives in that house. Obviously, she has seen all kinds of strange phenomena, such as a cigar shaped UFO that appeared here and there in the sky sometimes. She is really afraid of that, as it seemed to be getting closer in a few occasions. In a recent summer afternoon, although the sky was completely gray, the object was apparently really close, almost above the house. She stared at it and said: "-Do not come any nearer to me, come back Saturday and talk to the one who is looking for you!"(That means me...)As soon as she said that, it vanished. In other occasions, she reported a diamond shaped object hovering above the hill behind the house for a couple of minutes. It looks like they are interested in her. Maybe that is because she is too good for this world, she is constantly involved in charity such as giving her own things to the poor and helping sick and abandoned animals she finds in the streets. Many people consider her as some kind of local saint, she is greeted cheerfully wherever she goes, I have noticed that. This is unusual in any part of this world and the extraterrials notice that, too.

In one of those boring vigil nights when nothing happens at all, I arrived in their house at night with a bitter feeling of having wasted my time. As soon as I got there, I saw that Ms. Diva was washing the dishes deep in the night, because she suffered from a bad case of sleeplessness. As I said, the kitchen is just a part of the backyard covered by a roof, something usual in rural areas in Brazil. She seemed busy as usual and she began talking to me without really looking at me:

"-Are you waiting for that device from another world?" -She said.

"-Yes, Ma'am, I am!"-I said.

"-So, stay where you are, it will be coming anytime soon."-Then she left, with no signs of worry or surprise at all, and no more comments. By the time she said that it was 12h17min,the sky was clear and there was some moonlight. I thought she was joking.

Some 22 minutes later, at 12h39min, I saw the biggest UFO I have ever seen. (I will never forget that hour, although I do not remember the exact day, some Saturday night in July 2006). It was a huge lemon green disc with a long, brownish red fire trail behind it. It was about four times the size of a full moon. I had a feeling it was flying really low. It made no sound at all. I could only visualize it for some seconds, because it was flying towards the house roof and I could no longer see it after it passed that line. I ran to the other side of the house, but obviously, it was no longer visible. I believe it was a 200ft. wide thing, flying some 300ft. above me at an incredible speed, almost like a lightning.

After that, I had no more doubt Ms. Diva was a contactee somehow. I do not know for sure how aware she was of that, and she never talked about it more openly before or after that demonstration.

The sad moment of her passage to the other side occurred in the end of 2006,a difficult year for us all. She called each and every of her children in separate for a special talk. She announced she would be leaving this world in a month, and also gave advice to each son or daughter (she had four in total)and a painful goodbye hug. None of them dared to comment these talks to anyone else. And one month later she died of lung emphysema. Her corpse was then transferred to Sao Paulo crematorium under her request. Some minutes before she was cremated, Marcelo called me to come outside and see a silver UFO that was hovering at a distance. I guess they were saying goodbye or maybe honoring her last rites. I only saw it leaving, other people said it was very visible, but I was in tears and I saw it very blurred.

After she passed away UFO activity decreased steadily in that region, and we are now in a sort of low season. I confess that I got a little jealous, because I thought I was the main contactee around, but definitely I was NOT. It was her, Ms. Diva, down-to-earth as she was. How pretentious of me! Now I know they are less interested in me than I would like, but I also had my great moments with them.

MY FIRST ABDUCTION

My first abduction took place in August 2006. I have no doubt about it.

Once again, I was returning from an uneventful UFO vigil in a Saturday night. For years, I have neglected my social life and even my other activities just to go to a vigil every Saturday, whenever possible. Going there for nothing is rather frustrating. It is a long road and a total waste of my weekend time. Only if it rains hard or if the sky is too cloudy I end up staying in Sao Paulo, and that is something I do not appreciate at all. It is pretty much like gambling, there are days for winning and days for losing. I ate a sandwich and went to bed early that night.

Around 3 a.m., I guess, I started having a very odd dream. And a very lucid one, too.I saw an old man sitting at the porch of a typical U.S. house. it was obviously an American scene. The man sees an UFO and begins to run and shout in desperation, but a beam of light strikes him, and it beams him up in one of those solid light elevators. As he struggles in vain, he also senses a warm and pleasant feeling of levitation, and then he gives in. And for my surprise, as he feels that, I do too! I have never felt anything like this before, it was so good! I was sleeping and laughing.Have you ever done that? The levitation I felt was like a tickling massage, an absolute absence of bodily pains.

Later that night I began having another sequence of dreams, this time the scenery appeared to be a wedding party in Mexico. People were eating and talking loudly and there were mariachis playing their music. They were outside the house and a group of UFOs flew really low right above these people. They screamed and ran away. The UFOs in that dream produced an intense heat, just like sunshine, and once again I felt that heat! Dreams do not do that, dreams are mainly "vision and sound", at least for me. I never dream of tactile sensations such as sunshine heat. And once again, I found that funny and I laughed.

I woke up early the next day, and I automatically looked at the bathroom door that was on the right side and shouted: "-Get out of here, that is enough!" it was a weird reaction, I was waving my arms desperately and I fell down from bed, as some kind of retarded reaction to something. I wasn´t feeling scared or anything, I just did that without thinking or knowing why exactly. It felt as if I was frozen and then suddenly released and then I could finally move.There was nobody else around,it was around 8 a.m. but I felt tired the rest of the day and slept the whole afternoon and early that night.

In fact, I knew what that meant, and I scheduled an appointment with a hypnosis therapist I trust. He was familiar with the UFO and abduction topic, so he agreed to investigate that with me.He did all those things, that countdown, those words, and I got hypnotized pretty deeply.

In a certain moment he said: "-Now let´s go back to that Saturday night, the night of those strange dreams…"And I began to scream, struggled, grabbed his arm and said: "-Oh no, I can´t go there!"(He told me I sounded really scared to death).He made a magician-like gesture and said: "-Now, I remove all your fears, you are just telling me a story but you are not really there anymore…" and I calmed down. Then I kept talking in that typical slow, sleepy way:

"-There are three of them."

"-How do they look like?"-he asked.

"-Three gray aliens, the usual thing."-I said.

"-What is the purpose of their presence?

"-Medical exams."

"-Are all three doctors?"-He asked.

"-One is a doctor, the other two are bodyguards."(The doctor came in first, the two bodyguards were behind him, holding some kind of gun. The doctor held some rod with a bright green tip).

"-And how do they get in?"

"-They walked thorough the closed bathroom door." (Like a ghost. This was by far the most horrifying part of it, they cross solid walls and doors, and I do not believe a normal person can face this situation without panic).

"-And then?"-he asked.

"-They paralyzed me."

"-And after that?"-he asked again.

"-He made me levitate over my bed, three feet above my bed."(just like in that movie, "The exorcist")

"-And then?"(He did not have to speak much, the story was flowing well)

"-He examined me with that rod, above and under my body..." (That is why he made me levitate)

And this session went on, and there was another one, and the whole abduction scenario became crystal clear. The beings were indeed gray aliens, but not the short ones. They were somewhat taller, almost 6 feet tall, and they were wearing black tight clothes with green stripes in the arms. Their skin is ash grey, their heads unusually big, pear – shaped(an upside down pear, I mean) and the famous huge black eyes. No lips, their mouths were more like a cut, no visible noses, just nostrils. They walked normally. But the most striking detail was their hands because they looked like chicken paws with long sharp claws. Their hands were full of wrinkles and the overall appearance was quite threatening. However, I knew they meant no harm. By the way, they were there probably under my own request! But I could not help having fear. It is the animal side of us reacting against the unknown.

The alien doctor was carrying a suitcase and the rod which was a multiple use examining tool, but it also served to paralyze me. While he was passing the rod all over my body he could read all the data he needed about my health condition. I did not see what the guards were carrying very well. I was not able to scream or even move my head to see what they were doing. Strangely enough, they did not turn on the bedroom light but it was clear. Some people say that when someone is in astral projection, he may see everything at night just like if it was the bright light of day. Maybe I was a little out of my body, this is just a wild guess. Sincerely speaking, I do not know. The doctor talked to me telepathically, like aliens do, all the time. Even though he had no facial expression at all, I sensed his feelings of impatience and even anger because he thought I was misbehaving. He said:

"-You should not be scared. Someone who does what you do should know better. That is ridiculous. Behave yourself. Control yourself."He said that repeatedly: "-Behave yourself. Control yourself"

He went on with his exams. And he commented:

"-Your genetic constitution is awful. You were born to die young. You are decaying fast.You definitely do not apply for genetic improvement experiments. No procreation experiments using you. But you are a mental contact of ours. Therefore, I will fix you, so that you last a little longer."

As the being realized I was not getting any calmer, he showed disappointment. He pointed the rod at me and said: "-You'd better sleep now, dream that all you see now is just a dream." and then I had all those dreams about the old man and the Mexican wedding. They were just disguises for a real abduction taking place. I believe his original intention was to keep me awake during the process, but I showed no psychological structure for that. Before leaving, he said one last thing:

"-We will grant you a two year vacation. We will come back after you recover from this trauma."

That was back in 2006. UFO sightings and related experiences decreased a lot after that. Later vigils became a lot less interesting. On the other hand, my psychic abilities flourished steadily. Astral projections, premonitions became more frequent.Astral projections do not cause fear as much as abduction does, because the spirit cannot die, only the body can be destroyed. Only the body has self-defense mechanisms, animal instincts aiming at protecting life. The spirit can only live. He knows no death. And the spirit can go anywhere, fearleesly.

PARANORMAL ACTIVITY

After that abduction, psychic activity began to increase in my life. Those experiences are tremendously real and solid to me, even if I lived them in an altered state of consciousness. By "altered state" I mean something between asleep and awake, but highly interactive, where I can move my body and speak normally, but outside this physical body. I would call it "travelling without moving", the astral projection.

Some UFO researchers such as Prof. Laercio Fonseca in Brazil believe that gray aliens are responsible for the more physical abduction events because they are more adaptable to our planet and life form than other species. After a classical gray abduction, other species of alien beings can manifest themselves more easily and interact with humans more comfortably. This theory definitely applies to my case.

I was sleeping at night, at home, when I went somewhere else in astral projection, I would say. It was a room totally faced with white tiles, pretty much like a bathroom, really. Three short-haired blond men came in and bypassed me, without looking or greeting me at all. They were what people call "Nordic aliens" although they were shorter than I expected, just average. They had perfect skin and faces. They looked human. They did look like Germans or Scandinavians, and they were very icy and indifferent towards me. However, a strange energy or vibration emanated from them, and I knew I was not allowed to get any closer. The three looked like twins or clones, perfect copies of one another.I would say they looked young, in their mid twenties, and they were wearing solid white uniforms. They spoke telepathically to me, again with the same icy, superior air in their faces: "-We are the ones you are looking for. Here we are. We are what you expect to see. Today you will be submitted to psychological tests." They never made any eye contact, and they kept walking upstairs to some other room.

The so called "psychological test" was a series of visual situations where I saw people in pain or danger, for instance, a bleeding woman in a car crash accident or a group of hungry beggars, or a street fight between two gangs. I guess they were checking my potential for compassion and my tolerance to stress, my reaction to extreme situations.

At the end of this sequence, they called me to come upstairs to hear the verdict. For my great surprise, when I got upstairs all three of them were stark naked, sitting in a lotus position! Nevertheless they did not change that cold attitude towards me. They kept on avoiding eye contact and maintained that distant air. For a moment I thought this nudity could represent some erotic invitation, but their motionless indifference told me otherwise. Maybe they just enjoyed nakedness, pretty much like naturists. One of them said mentally:

"-You failed. You are much too aggressive. You are of no use for us. No way."

And so the experience ended and I woke up sweating cold with a strange chill all over my body. I did not sleep well the rest of that night, but nothing else happened.

Probably, they continued to observe me afterwards, in many different occasions. One day I went to school to apply a test to an upper middle class boy, G.C., and he seemed very nervous about it. As a matter of fact, he cried. I think he had a very demanding father. I tried to calm him down, but nothing worked, and I decided to give him some answers, so that he would achieve a passing grade easily. After I finished, I told everybody in the teachers room how spoiled he was and we all made cruel jokes about him.

In the same night, around 1 a.m., I felt a sticky cold hand grabbing my foot. I opened my eyes and a saw a figure totally made of flames and hollow in the middle. I shrank and shivered in absolute horror and there was nowhere to go. The being said:

"-You laughed about the young human's fear, by the time of his test. So, that is your test now.Laugh! C'mon, laugh out loud!

The being disappeared immediately after that and I have felt indescribable fear, like I have never felt before. If he stayed longer, I think I would have died. He came just to teach me a lesson. Do not mess with them, there is no lying to aliens and spiritual beings. With experiences like that, it is to be expected that I became insomniac, practically sleeping with one eye opened.Over the years, I got to the point of getting sick because of that.

The next experience I would call it "Contactees school". In this event, I was in an empty white room, surrounded by young Earthlings. They all seemed to be below 18 years of age, and they were normal in every sense. But they were special in their intelligence, you may call then "indigo" children if you like, they had a different shine in their eyes. They came closer to me and said:

"-This is the contactee training center. We were brought here in order to discuss our experiences so that we may understand them better and accept our condition more easily. You are the oldest one today, such things usually start earlier. (Alien contact, he meant)

One of those kids brought a black iron box and he turned it on.It was some kind of machine. A whole sequence of colorful beams came out of it. Of course, each color represented a function, but I did not have the faintest idea what could they be. He asked if I knew how to handle it, and I honestly said I did not. Then he commented: "-Great. That is lesson number one. Never pretend to know something you do not know!"End of that experience.

In another occasion, I saw the same group of kids in a room that seemed perfectly normal at first, but there was a big brown circle on a wall, some kind of flat screen. They pointed at it and said: "-if you want to visit our base, stare at that circle, wishing that this room moves forward, and it will move in its direction. After that, they left.

I obviously wanted to visit that base so much, and I was curious and scared at the same time. I looked deeply into that brown circle, and it became something like a TV screen and I could see the forest and I realized that room was actually moving forward. It went on and on until it finally stopped in a given moment. As soon as the room stopped, I began to hear steps from a corridor behind me. I was shivering with fear, I was wondering what kind of being would it be this time. The alien being this time looked pretty much like a normal man, dressed almost like a doctor, with a white duster and gray pants underneath. His eyes were cold and I did not really trust him, despite of his human appearance. Then he showed me a metal table and asked me to lie down on it. I obeyed, and a bunch of those teenagers surrounded me then. He started introducing some implants under my skin, and the procedure involved little cuts that I considered painful. I asked for anesthetics, but he paid no attention to me. Since I wanted to get out of this situation, suddenly I went out of my body, as in an astral projection inside another astral projection. Then he said: "-You see (to the teenagers), if a person resists to the out-of-the-body experience, pain is a little push that will force him or her to do so." I hated him for saying so. Then the experience ended, I woke up in my bed.

Apart from those alien contact experiences, there were many others of a different kind. I had many encounters with deceased people. Such experiences usually start in an empty room, and there is always another room. I never see what is inside that other room. Typically, a deceased person would come out of that other room and greet me in the room where I am staying. I guess the reason for that is the materialization process, which can be quite scary. They only show the materialization when it is ready even if it is only a "dream", they do not want to turn it into a nightmare. The ones I call "guides" are two, a man with blue eyes and a woman with red hair and wearing glasses. They both look young ,say, in their mid-thirties and perfectly normal.

In the first of such experiences I met my aunt Yara and her husband Joao, as well as my grandfather Jacob. They all passed away more than ten years ago. The red-haired doctor told me I should wait in a room for a dearest relative who was in another room. She asked me: "-Who would you like to meet today? Someone you miss a lot?" And I thought of my aunt, I did not know she was there. The woman said: "-Now, go to the other room, she is waiting." And so it was, my aunt Yara was there with her arms wide open, and she said: "-C'mon, dear one, give me a hug!"

As soon as I saw that, my uncle Joao intervened, and he said: "-Do not cry, do not get too emotional, otherwise you will interrupt this transmission.' But she called me the names she used to when I was a child and I began to cry. The experience was immediately interrupted, I woke up in my bed, and I kept on crying for quite a while. And that was it.

Some time later, I was once again in one of those rooms where I met a former student of mine. She embraced me from behind, and she had long, beautiful hands which I immediately recognized. She said: "-Surpriiiiiiiiiise!" But she did not let me see her face. It was a brief experience and it ended that way. Some days later, I asked another student of mine if he had seen this woman recently, because they worked in the same bank. This man, my student, showed great surprise and asked: "-Don´t you know that she passed away one year ago? She was depressed and she went to the top of her building and jumped." I guess this is the reason why she did not let me see her face, she was probably still disfigured. I believe it takes a while before the spiritual body is healed from the trauma of death.

Later that year, I saw my grandfather dressed in the 1940's fashion and looking very young. He actually died in 1973, when I was 6 years old. When I saw him, I had a very strange reaction nobody expected. I grabbed him by his collar and said angrily: "-You all are in a place where you know more about extraterrial beings than I do. Tell me a little of what you already know!" The red haired woman appeared immediately and told me to stop.She said:

"-This is the time for meeting your dear ones. If you wish to know about aliens, ask the ones who were just like you are today. Ask the ones who dedicated their lives to that. Not everyone is interested in that. Stop that nonsense!' And the experience was interrupted.

Looking back at that experience, I think she referred to Osni Schwarz, my UFO research friend from young days, or maybe another researcher I had not met personally, such as General Uchoa or someone like that. Any ideas?

Little by little those spiritual guides teach me how to behave properly in their world. Sometimes I remember entire moments, sometimes, just fragments. The blue eyed guide called those rooms "intermediate zones", where the two dimensions meet. Once I grabbed his hand and said: "-That is amazing, your hand is solid and warm, even though you are dead!"

To which he replied angrily: "-Don´t you ever call me DEAD again. You are dead to me, because we live in two worlds set apart. Nevertheless you are alive, and so am I! So you´d better say we live in different dimensions. Or if you prefer, you can say different densities. This is your nr. 1 lesson in good manners over here.That is very offensive."

Experiences with deceased people are never as scary as experiences with aliens. Deceased people are exactly the same as us, we can relate to their words and reactions. I would talk to them the same way I would talk to you. Aliens are different, they evolved in another path and they talk and behave in a way we would consider illogical. Besides, they have a strange vibration. It is hard to describe it, some strange electricity or radiation, not to mention their appearance. Whenever I see a human looking alien, yet I know it is not really human, because of that unmistakable vibration.

There is another amazing experience; I would call it "a visit to the gray base". In this specific experience, I woke up lying on a stone bed, and looking all around, I realized everything was made of excavated solid rock. Everything was cut and polished to perfection; there were tables, seats, doors. I had a feeling it was Earth, but some hidden place underground. I saw my arms, they were skinny and grayish. I also had those chicken paws for hands. I had been turned into a gray alien! Besides, I was surrounded by many of them, and they did not look at me, something as if I was completely normal. Only one of them spoke to me mentally, as it follows:

"-Welcome to our base. We turned you into one of us, so that you can walk around unnoticed. Enjoy your tour."-After that, I began to wander in that place, going from room to room. There was some funny elevator which rotated and opened its door in a different room each time, a very strange thing. Apart from that, the sequence of rooms was pretty boring. Nothing there was particularly beautiful or interesting. They were doing their job, walking and nothing else. I had a feeling they were naked, their skinny bodies were the color of an elephant. One of them turned to me and said:

"-You wouldn´t like to live here. We live in a perfectly equalitarian society. You do not wish to be equal with others: you are willing to distinguish from others. You are the kind of being who wishes to be unique. There are two possibilities for evolution. Evolution towards equality or evolution towards differentiation. Not for you, thus."I still meditate over this comment. After all,do we really enjoy equality?

And some time after that I met that blond alien again. But this time he came alone, there was only one of them. And he was not naked this time.On the contrary, he was wearing a long black gown similar to a Catholic priest´s robe. His hands were in a prayer position, and he came along with another human-looking being. She looked completely like a Peruvian native or something like that and she was equally dressed in a black robe. I would never guess she was not human if I saw her on the streets of Brazil, where there are many people who look pretty much like that. The whole place was rather rustic, just like a primitive fortress made of stone and wood, not the hi-tech thing we tend to imagine.I looked at the "Peruvian" being and commented: "-Oh my, she is so human-looking, I would never tell her from a perfectly normal Latin American native."

As soon as I said that, she moved backwards and covered her face in horror because of my proximity. I was very insulted by her gesture. I asked the blond guy the reason for that strange reaction. After all, why was I so disgusting to her? To which he replied:

"-She looked deeply into you and she saw your past lives and your ultimate nature and she realized your bestiality, a bestiality that is unusual, even among human beings on Earth. I have already gotten used to you but she is seeing you for the very first time. She is startled by what she has just seen."

Sincerely speaking, I do not think I am that bad. There are much worse people everywhere. Anyway, this being could see beyond, right into my akashic files and see my deeds in distant past lives of which I do not recall. My present existence is a pretty boring and ordinary one. And so he went on:

Today is your oath day. Within a few moments you will see a group of humans leaving the big ceremony hall, then it will be your turn. Those humans are many, they wear white with an orange stripe.Due to your amazing bestiality, you will swear your oath dressed all in blach with a brown stripe. Only three other humans are in a similar situation and the three of you will do the same. This small group of unusually brutal beings is perfect for some functions."

Then a big door opened, and a happy group of humans came out, talking about the oath and smiling. The blond man and the "Peruvian" alien walked into that room first, I followed them. The big room looked like an ancient Greek theater. There were two other human beings there, a man and a woman. Both were wearing a black robe with a brown stripe, standing in the middle of a stage. There were many other beings watching the oath scene. A "Nordic" alien was presiding the ceremony, I still remember him but I do not recall what he said, this was somehow erased from my memory. Therefore, I do not know what I said. And I do not know for sure whether I accepted it or not. This happens sometimes, it is like my spirit had heard it, but my material consciousness did not. In other words, I was not allowed to know what they said there.

There are many other similar experiences along the way. I will not describe them.Otherwise it would get too boring. And there is no way I can prove such spiritual events, for they are spiritual. What makes me believe in them is its logic and sense. They are totally different from a normal dream or hallucination. I dream every night and I can tell the difference. These experiences are clearly interconnected, and they relate to one another like a puzzle with pieces that match perfectly.

THE STRANGER AT THE BUS STATION

In one of those Sunday mornings, I was returning to Sao Paulo after a pretty dull UFO vigil. I was taking the 8 o'clock bus from Sao Pedro, where I stayed over after the vigil. I took a taxi and I got off in front of that small town station.

As soon as I arrived, a smiling man opened the taxi door for me. He greeted me as if he had known me for ages. But I had never seen him before. At first I thought he was a beggar. But he was elegantly dressed and good looking too. He seemed to be in his mid thirties, and behaved as if we were good friends. I was a little scared, because I thought he was crazy and I did not know what to do or what to say. So I pretended to know him and smiled back. I had bought the ticket the previous day, so all I had to do was sit and wait for my bus. He sat next to me and started to talk. He said straight away:

"-I know why you are here. You are after **them**. They have a base in this area. You know, you smell like aliens. You are totally involved in this thing."

I was startled to hear that. I remained in silence and let him talk.He went on:

"-I like you very much. I admire you for what you do. You know, some years ago I was in a rural resort hotel in Monte Verde(MG) when I got out of my cottage at night and I saw a big green UFO over it. I was horrified, at the same time I was thrilled. I knew they were there to invite me in, and I accepted that offer. The first moments are really terrible, but when you are into the ship, you relax and feel great. There is nothing else left to do than enjoying it. A wonderful experience. And you want more and more of it. We are two of a kind. And, meanwhile, you learn wonderful things."

I was confused. I just nodded in agreement. He continued:

"One of these days, after being taken a few times, they will show you something in a special occasion. They will show you what you have done wrong in order to deserve this birth in a planet like this (Earth).A terrible crime you committed was the reason for this sad human condition you are facing now. Believe me, it was something really bad, otherwise you wouldn't be here. The day you realize your evil deeds, you will feel so ashamed that you will hide your face. You would rather not know what you have done. You will miss your days of sweet ignorance. But there is no turning back. This is about to happen."

He invited me to stay in that town and go back to the fields. Stupid me, I was afraid of him and I turned down his invitation. I said my bus had arrived and so I needed to go. He held my hand and said:

"-It is a pity. I have great admiration for you ,and I know you will find what you have been looking for."

Oh my, I regret that mistake so much... I left and I have never seen him again, of course. And I do not really know what he really was, a contactee, an alien, a clone or what. These questions will remain unanswered forever, I think.

TRYING TO UNDERSTAND THE EXPERIENCES

As time goes by, I understand more and more what is going on with me and about UFOs as a whole. Firstly, the "no photography" issue. Why are pictures not allowed during a vigil? Most UFOs vanish as soon as we turn on a digital camera or any other recording device. Is an experience "for eyes only". Not only governments are hiding the truth, they too, the aliens, are hiding the truth and apparently avoiding open contact.

By not allowing pictures and many other kinds of physical evidence, aliens select naturally the ones who really believe, separating them from others who are just seeking evidence.They are excluding skeptics in general,intentionally. If there were enough of really undeniable evidence everywhere, the "believe it or not" factor would disappear. It would be another proven scientific factor, just like dinosaurs, or the existence of the stars above us. The present situation allow us a choice, which is being interested in UFO and aliens or not. And the ones who believe are constantly tested by an annoying lack of events or evidence. We all wish to see and prove a lot more. But that is not the way they chose to do things.

Another reason for allowing pictures is protecting the witnesses/contactees from opposing groups, such as governments and some fundamentalist religious groups which are willing to destroy evidence just to keep their dogmas alive. If a given person had too much evidence alone, he would be an easy target for those. Or he could claim to be the ultimate bearer of the truth, the spokesman of the alien gods and impose his or her beliefs based on that. Or simply, this person could be captured by government intelligence agencies and disappear. In fact, every contactee receives messages from alien beings, but he distorts them naturally, according to his opinions, beliefs and level of understanding. Considering the telepathic nature of those messages, there is no way one would not alter them while writing or talking about it. Luring human beings for a spontaneous search for contact is more valuable than the message itself, I believe. And everyone is free to accept or deny the UFO reality.

The so called "mystic ufology" mentions the "Nordic" alien Ashtar Sheran and the Shan mind wave transmitted from his spaceship. The Shan would be an awareness wave capable of intensifying people's interest in spiritual, environmental, cosmic, social awareness and so on. It could speed up evolution, as "Shan" is the name he gives to planet Earth itself, a vibration dedicated to its planetary progress. Despite of being sent equally to all human beings all over the world, the way people receive and interpret it will differ from person to person. There will be no two equal responses to it on the entire planet Earth. That is why contactees do not convey the same messages. As a matter of fact, so many alien messages sound silly or conventional because that is the nature of its human receiver. Unfortunately it is so.

Isis and I never completely agreed in terms of what is the right approach concerning UFOs and aliens. That does not mean we could not work together and coexist despite of our differences. This is beautiful. She is more of a scientific kind, and I am more of a spiritualistic kind whenever we talk about this phenomena. For instance, I have been a vegetarian for 25 years, and she does not believe that this could influence our chances for UFO observation, but I do. Due to my long term involvement with Buddhism, I practice the Vipassana meditation, and I use it as a warm up activity for my vigils too. I also believe in the importance of maintaining sexual abstinence in the vigil day, in order to accumulate certain kundalini energy within yourself. No drugs or alcoholic beverages allowed. I do not think this is a mere superstition.

I also believe that the way you lead your life matters a lot. Being generous, spreading goodwill, charity, will have an influence in your results during a UFO vigil. It gives you "credits". It increases our psychic powers, our openness to the universe. And it increases your chances of success in UFO vigil, too. There is nothing wrong with that, we all must give and take, nobody needs nothing. But we must choose the ones who are going to give and take from us. It is a waste if you spend our energies with the ones who do not deserve that. Our intuition shows if we receive as much as we give or not, but we sometimes ignore our feelings. For instance, many times I made huge efforts to bring people to the vigils with me, but they were not really interested. I gave the best of myself to others for nothing. A total waste of time. So I began to focus on the already existing group. I tried hard to develop patience and tolerance towards the ones who are also group members, even if they think or behave in a way I do not agree or approve. I try to talk more patiently, more carefully, in a more generous way. This is hard for me. I am hot-headed, short tempered, moody, greedy, and sometimes poisonous in my comments. Reducing that is exactly what aliens expect that I do. This is part of what they call being less aggressive and evolving.

In the beginning I thought that being vegetarian and meditating would be enough to foster contact. Therefore, I tried to convince others to do the same. But they belonged to other religions or cultural backgrounds than mine, and I felt disappointed about that. Even so, they had countless UFO experiences on their own, without doing the things I thought they should do. That made me wonder if my beliefs were the right ones. Well, they are right for me, not for everybody. Developing tolerance to the differences among us is what really matters. I do not need to agree with everything, but I must respect everyone. It seems like aliens notice the internal atmosphere among the UFO research group members. I do not believe they are interested in a broken group where everybody dislikes everybody else.

There is such a huge search for UFO related sites in the internet nowadays,but most people are not really willing to spend a Saturday night out there in the cold waiting for a UFO. It is amazing how passive people are concerning this topic. They prefer to learn from hearsay. I think fear is the main reason why people do not try a real UFO vigil. Due to all these horrifying stories of gray abduction everywhere, they stay indoors. This disinformation tactics seem to be working really well, increasing the "fear of a negative experience". For the ones who still participate in those UFO vigils, the only thing to be really afraid of is the boredom of an eventless night. Morale gets low when there is a long quiet period, when the skies are silent.

Even in such bad times when nothing happens, there are many other related events. Receiving mental messages is one of them. They cling to my mind. I hear the same sentence repeatedly, until I finally internalize the message. Here are some examples that I jotted down:

"-Mental contact starts in the mind" (There is no use going to a vigil with a foul mind)

"-Loving the animals" (That is ironic, because there are so many reports of animal mutilation, but I hope they only do it if absolutely necessary).

"-These beings do not only know you."(Do not be conceited about your alien contact, you are one among many others)

"-We do not teach this to beginners" (Everything must be taught in the right moment)

"-Good not to be fake" (The beauty of sincerity, especially in a telepathic world)

"-Doubt is contempt" (In a way, skeptic people show their contempt towards UFO believers by questioning them so ruthlessly)

"-We are important brothers" (Any doubt about that?)

"-You will be persecuted"(If you insist on talking about UFOS and things like that)

"-Do what must be done" (Do not hesitate, be bold)

"-We will meet in the appointed time for a visit" (The importance of establishing a specific time and location for UFO vigils and keep it regularly)

"-There is not only one possibility for the future" (It can be changed, yes!)

"-The abductee will sleep now" (Creepy....)

"You are afraid" (Of course I am)

"-Eradicate" (All impurities within your heart)

These advices were straight to the point and very meaningful by the time they had been given to me. They are sometimes pretty obvious, but they often state the obvious again, so that I realize simple things that I had been overlooking. Simple instructions for me and for mankind as a whole. Things like "-Clean you mind", "-Eradicate your impurities", and so on. They keep playing inside my head like a radio with a repetitive message. Sometimes these messages are more like a conversation, they are more complex. Just like that inner voice we all have, the voice that speaks to us internally. But I sense it is not really me, it is somebody else. I ask myself whether it is an alien or some human spirit. It could be both, or maybe they take turns.

They talk about this world and comment on it. They often talk about this world and its religions. They say religions nowadays have become an obstacle to progress in many aspects. Do you know John Lennon's song "Imagine":"-Imagine there are no religions, too"? At first I disagreed frontally, I had been a devoted Buddhist for many years, but later I began to accept that idea. I watch the news and see so many horrible things done in the name of religion. For being dogmatic, people do things that do not make sense in the world today. Some of these things are unacceptable to the ones who are not members of that specific religion, but its followers behave is if they were blind.

A good example is homophobia. Many religious authorities condemn homosexuality, but they do not really have a good explanation for that. They just do it because "It is written"in their texts. Or they place women in a lower rank because it has always been this way, or they claim this is the natural order of things. Or they treat animals badly, because their religion says they are at their disposal. Even worse, they treat the entire planet badly, because they believe they are protected by God who would have given them this world for whatever suits them best. They say "-My world", "-Our world, given to us by God". Is it really yours? Or are you just a temporary tenant? Many other existed here before you, both individuals and species alike, and others shall eventually come in the future to replace you.

Such dogmatic thoughts are tremendously dangerous. What if a religious group suggests not using condoms in a poor African country and they get AIDS as a consequence of such advice? How can this be seen as goodness? Or if a religious group opposes contraceptives in an overpopulated, impoverishing world as we have now, how can this be considered wise? Such sexual moral values have been established some two thousand years ago in a totally different world. And so many people follow these rules without knowing really why. Outdated ideas that can no longer fit in our world lead to hypocrisy and double standards, emphasizing the wrong directions that lead this world to a confusing situation. That does not mean religions are worthless, but they must be recycled and reinterpreted, like everything else.

The hippie movement and counterculture as a whole were symptoms of this need for change. Extraterrials have an influence in that direction, they hope we are willing to change what must be changed, fearlessly. They obviously expect that we open our minds in order to accept the new realities to come. Like their existence, for instance, but not only that. If the scriptures do not explain certain things, than we must search in more contemporary sources, instead of denying the new facts. An open contact with aliens would demand such reforms, a spiritual reform prior to actual contact, not after. That is exactly what is delaying the open contact.

Another important thing is the need for more birth control. The human life expectancy has been extended, medicine advanced, and birth control did not come along. People have three, four, five children, based on their freedom of choice, unaware of the environmental impact of it. Planet Earth is really not that big. That is a very thorny issue for any government, but it has to be addressed. There should be a much smaller population in this world than there is today, and we can reduce it gradually. People who opt for an only child or no children are helping to save the biosphere and for that they give up the joys of parenthood. This can be seen as a high form of altruism.

I do not agree with the idea that aliens are primarily concerned about our wars. They have always existed, and violence in more primitive worlds is no surprise to them.Nowadays they are more concerned about the relatively slow, but steady destruction of Earth´s environment by pollution and overpopulation. Mankind's lack of interest towards the environment is amazing for them, because we do not travel to other planets regularly, so we do not have anywhere else to go. Most people do not hold themselves responsible for weather changes. They talk almost as if the did not live here. They even play dumb, by asking questions like "-Unusual weather this year, don´t you think?"Or, "-Why is it so hot today?"People want to go no like this until the end. They hope some future government will face this music.

Mankind will not be allowed to explore other planets, not even the neighboring Mars or the Moon. Aliens occupy them with their own bases and they know how nasty we are. They manage hostile environments easily and they excavate solid rock to build their compounds totally underground and safe from external trouble. In many planets there are no surface cities which are more vulnerable. For that reason, we do not see where they live. That includes remote areas on planet Earth itself. Aliens may help us in many aspects of our lives, such as medicine and electronic equipments, but never our space programs. This is simply not allowed. That is exactly one of the factors that upset our governments and it will not change anytime soon.

It is clear to me that aliens do not judge us morally. They would not interfere directly just because we behave in a way they disapprove. War, injustice, discrimination, hypocrisy, exploitation.This is none of their business, this is our business. If we live like that, it is ok for them. They are not willing to teach us how to live. In fact, many things are expected to be so, considering our level of evolution.

Earthlings must learn how to do better by themselves, although aliens sometimes whisper a solution in our ears. But aliens are the gardeners of the universe; they will not let us destroy this biosphere whimsically. They observed for centuries the way we lived, maybe improving things a little in a not so noticeable way. But if we threaten the biosphere too much, they will permit catastrophes in order to slow down mankind's rampaging technological civilization. The so called "doomsday" is nothing but nature reacting to our aggression in the same way. Tsunamis, floods, droughts ,fire, plagues, starvation are the weapons used by nature.

Aliens have witnessed human cruelty and ignorance for centuries, in silence, just like a biologist observes a lion in the savannah. Whenever a technological civilization arises, they become more attentive to it. As a matter of fact, to a certain extent, they allowed it to happen. They keep an eye on it, checking if it is growing in a sustainable way or not. We are mere tenants, not the owners of any world. Little by little, they are speeding up our biological evolution, transitioning from Homo Sapiens to a more sophisticated being. This is one of the purposes of the hybridization program. We do not notice this transition, the external difference between Homo Sapiens and the new species to come is not so evident, but the mental improvement will be remarkable. This is what many people call "indigo children", born from normal human parents but radically more intelligent than they were. They will be less emotional, more logical and capable of a broader understanding of things, less concerned about protecting their own family in opposition to the rest of society or the planet. In more advanced planets, the very concept of family no longer exists, as aliens substitute a worn-out, aging body for a brand new one. And this new body receives a download of information of his user's past life and knowledge in general. Therefore, many aliens refer to their peers as "my class", or "my people", but never as "my family", because they do not have one. Their species is their family, their planet is their home.

I AM KRAAKAR

This is by far the most important and controversial part of this book. It is based on experiences I had. Experiences of astral projection that took place after the first abduction and the encounter with a strange man in the bus station. These experiences were investigated with the help from hypnosis regression therapy. Some were so crystal clear to me that nothing else was necessary.

Many times at night I wake up with a strange feeling, something between being awake and sleeping. This usually happens around 3 a.m., probably because that is the best time for spiritual experiences. When that happens, I see colors and shapes, circles, squares, patterns and so on. And when I start sleeping again, I have unusually lucid images, pretty much like a movie. Stories that make sense. Not like a dream. I can even smell and touch things in these occasions. It feels like a TV show, transmitted from somewhere.

The very first of those experiences happened some three years ago.In this experience, I was in a kind of fortress with thick black walls. It was warm and the air was clean. Its rooms were decorated with a most stunning collection of art works from different historic periods imaginable, such as Louis XV furniture of the best kind, Chinese vases, everything you can see in a top notch museum. There was a door at the back of the room I was in, and a reptilian female came out of it. She had an ash gray skin and black eyes on both sides of her head, pretty much like a lizard from planet Earth. I saw no scales, and her facial features resembled pretty much a brontosaurus. It did not correspond to the depictions of reptilians I had seen in books and movies. Her eyes were in each side of the head, not in the front, like I saw in many pictures everywhere. She had a huge mouth similar to a modern iguana. I could see a long string of small teeth in it that looked like a saw, and a sharp tongue. She had a friendly and majestic air, a natural elegance in her movements. But that was not the most incredible. She was wearing human garments. She was wearing an exquisite Japanese kimono in black silk with cherry blossoms in pink! It could not be more surreal. All those objects from planet Earth belonged to them, although they were clearly not of their making. It was some kind of collection. She began talking to me, again telepathically:

"-Your name is Kraakar. I am so sorry for you. I regret your condition today. We expect patiently for the day of your return. Your return to us and to your real beauty. Now, take that mirror and see what your real beauty is like. And remember later."

As soon as she said that, she gave me a small mirror and I could see myself. And I was similar to her. There were small differences, I was greener and my head was more like the head of a tyrannosaurus. When I saw my body, I realized I was wearing human clothes too. In my case they were rich Indian silk robes with heavy jewelry on the top of it. This made the whole scene look like a fairy tale, reptiles dressed up to the hilt. I had clear feeling all that gorgeous collection was the result of piracy or smuggling from planet Earth. They definitely did not pay VAT taxes. It was obvious they enjoyed these products and collected them somehow. They purchased, stole or traded them from somewhere. It reminded me of the British Empire and the collections they accumulated during their incursions to the colonies such in India or Africa, and the museums they built out of them.If we consider human history,especially

European colonialism, this is nothing new. It was all very bizarre, and I am telling you all that, and I know it is hard to believe, but I am not willing to hide details of my experiences.

The second similar experience explains the first. I saw a strange looking bald man. The setting of this experience is a Biblical city. He stares at me and asks:

"-Do you believe that Sodom was destroyed because people there enjoyed anal sex, or because they were homosexuals?"

I replied: "-Most definitely not, I think this is a myth created to condemn homosexuality."

"-That is absolutely right"-he said. "That is why I tell you something really serious was going on over there back then, and you were directly involved in it. Look."

I saw an old citadel from thousands of years ago, the typical Biblical image. His voice said:

"-Now, here we are, 24 hours before the great destruction of the city of Sodom.'

It looked the way you would expect, stone walls, animals, people dressed in long gowns. On the top of the city there was a walled court. In this court there were many alien spacecrafts parked all over the place. And there was also a counter, where reptilian beings were doing business with humans from those days. The reptilians were trading off objects of their making for raw materials such as gold, precious stones and metals in general. In return, they offered medications, but also addictive drugs and weapons. Therefore they were smuggling or at least trading illegally with primitive humans.

I realized I was once again that reptilian being called Kraakar.Next to me, there was a younger reptilian which I regarded as a disciple or assistant. He looked at me and spoke very candidly to me:

"-Captain Kraakar, you are too corrupt. How can you possibly expect that we will do all that and remain unnoticed? The Confederation of Planets will find out this irregularity pretty soon. You are dealing technological artifacts with primitive beings and making them dependent on us. That is total infringement of all cosmic laws. We can´t go far with that."

My, or Kraakar's answer was: "-Don´t worry, we will leave soon, before they arrive."

And that was not all. Kraakar was not only trading illegally, but he was also creating hybrids. There were many weird beings walking all over the place, odd mixtures of human beings with animals, such as dogs, bulls, crabs, insects, all mixed up in a very nasty and illegal genetic experiment. These beings were created in order to generate subspecies that could be useful in the future, as well as threatening those primitive humans with creatures that matched their mythology and their deepest fears. Sumerian art frequently depicts those beings, and archeologists today interpret that as sheer fantasy. But it was more real than one can imagine today, in the alien quarters. And that goes not only for reptilians.These experiments were widely practiced among aliens in general.

Suddenly the hybrids began to die. They simply dropped dead for no apparent reason. Then Kraakar asked his little assistant: "-Who is killing my experiments?'

And the little reptilian said: "-Just look up there in the sky..."

There it was a gigantic ship in the shape of a silver ring. The hollow area in the middle of the ring was a portal through which Confederate fighters came down in large groups. Those little fighters exterminated mercilessly every human being in that place with the infamous "rain of fire". Not sent by God really, but by the Confederation of Planets.They decided to erase this event from the face of the Earth completely. Future generations would not have a clue of what was really going on over there.

Ironically, all reptilians involved were kept alive, since they deserved a fair judgment. It is funny to imagine that humans should die immediately, although they were mere victims of the reptilian seduction. No one of them could survive to tell the story, except Lot, but I do not know anything about that.Confederation of Planets jurisdiction demands that outlaws should not be executed before judgement.

The humans who were exterminated, on the other hand would reincarnate in new bodies, in a totally new life, unaware of what they did or saw in Sodom. They forget past lives, so they can start all over again in a different time and place, free from the bad habits of a previous existence. Therefore the Confederation of Planets did not need to worry much about them.

Alien beings, reptilian or not, remember their previous existences. They retain full memory of their knowledge from the former life. A simple execution for them would not mean much. They would be reborn exactly the same. They would simply receive a new body to repeat the same behaviors.

After the city was totally erased by fire, as the Bible describes, no humans were left to tell the story of this reptilian-human trade. This problem was solved, and now it was time for the judgment. A jury of human looking Nordic aliens was there to judge. The courtroom looked a bit like a Greek theater with its semicircular benches. The reptiles would stand in the middle, immobilized. The Confederates looked at us with scorn.Everybody knew the punishment would be as dire as possible.

The reptilian ambassadress was present in order to plead for the reptilian bandits. She looked divine, in that long, heavily embroidered white gown, definitely a female of high position. The scene was in every way similar to international court cases on Earth today, she was there to protect her citizens, no matter how wrong they were. But no one was moved by her appeals. The verdict was proclaimed:

"-Captain Kraakar, what you did is really unforgivable. The punishment for that is the worst we can imagine. You will be reborn in the planet you tried to ruin. You will spend some thousands of years reincarnating in this miserable human form, this painful, primitive form of existence, until you finally regenerate."

Planet Earth used to be, and still is seen as a prison for alien criminals. There is no better correction for a nasty alien than a rebirth in a world like this. Watching the slow evolution of a difficult planet in its infancy is hard. Experiencing its unfair social organization, experiencing painful aging and early death is almost unbearable. Living 70 or 80 years for them is preposterous, a small fraction of their normal life span. And in ancient times, life would have been even harder and shorter. Intelligence and merit are often ignored, and privilege and caste rule such primitive societies. Truth rarely prevails. In short, Earth is a world of pain. The equivalent to the idea of hell for them.

To advanced aliens in general, there is no death. When their bodies no longer suit their needs, they change it for a new one, just like some sort of plastic surgery. The new body is usually similar to the previous one. Their knowledge and experiences from previous existences are transferred to the brand new body, together with the soul that remains in a container while the body transfer takes place. Other species have abandoned material form altogether, but that is another level of evolution. Being reborn in a "natural" world like Earth, where the natural sequence of life, growth, aging and death still prevails is a terrible punishment. Humans, like other primitive species, do not remember their previous reincarnations, the languages they spoke in previous lives or anything useful from their former existences. They are born ignorant, they do not know where they come from or where they are going to. Their evolutionary stage could not bear this kind of information. Nature is wise in doing so. If they remembered the previous lives, they would remember essentially pain, impermanence, disease, separation. Aging itself is seen as a disease for aliens. Therefore they do not need prisons or mental institutions. They throw misbehaved individuals in worlds like Earth. And they learn how to behave the hard way.

The reptilian ambassadress claimed that the outlaws were trying to be real patriots who were willing to bring more wealth to the magnificent Reptilian Empire settled in Orion. It did not convince anybody. This is not the first time such things had happened. This group of pirates was not receiving orders from anybody. They were simply doing what they felt like. That was an obvious infringement of non-interference treaties. An action that could have been incredibly harmful to primitive mankind. Many other similar illegal groups were molesting innocent and equally primitive races in undeveloped planets. The Confederation of planets was well aware of that.

I did not see what happened next. I guess we were executed, and our souls were locked up in some kind of container, which is pretty much like a bottle, to be unlocked in the right place. This place was Earth. Somehow, they manage to keep a consciousness-soul locked in a jar and release it in the place where it is supposed to reincarnate.

Strangely as it sounds, a soul is attracted by the gravity of a planet in the moment of conception. This soul will be pushed into a womb because in that moment it can not fly away, due to gravitational attraction. This is probably the origin of stories in the Arabic book "One Thousand and One Nights" where the genius gets stuck in a lamp and asks someone to open it so that he can be free. This not only fantasy, this is a reality in terms of alien technology. Therefore, the reptilian bandits' souls were poured into the Earth's field of energy so that they would be captured by it. On Earth, the exile planet, they would live as perfectly normal humans, and that meant experiencing their habitual sufferings.

The reptilian ambassadress did not succeed in pleading not guilty for the bandits, but at least she was granted the right to follow up on them from a distance during their multiple existences on Earth. By doing so, they could be protected a little, just a little. As humans, they could no longer do much evil.They became fragile, just like any other human being. Thus they became harmless to the Confederation of Planets and the universe. There is no better form of imprisonment.

PAST LIVE MEMORIES

After this experience, they showed what happened to me in my earthly human existences. As you know, my arrival was not the most honorable. Sodom was destroyed between 2000BC and 1000BC.That is between three and four thousand years ago. This is not much for aliens; they remember very well what I did and who I was. They have it all recorded. And there are no unfair trials in alien court, because they are telepathic, so there is no lying.

I have fragmentary memories of those lives. Spiritual guides do not allow us to uncover what is too painful and disturbing. What we see is what we can bear. That depends exclusively on each person's spiritual and mental evolution. I do not believe that past life therapy is dangerous at all, I learned a lot about myself by exploring those fragments of memory that came out of hypnosis sessions combined with astral projections. It showed who I am and how I got here. How can this be a bad thing?

Aren't we all looking for more awareness? I know I might be misled by false memories, but this can happen to anyone. There are no warranty certificates for beliefs.

These memories originated from astral projections that I had deep in the night, combined with hypnosis sessions afterwards. The hypnosis session clarifies the fragmentary images. I can not prove them with archeological evidence. I will show them in chronological order rather than the order they appeared to me.

The very first experience I recall was in Ancient Egypt. That was a good one. I was a great priest. I still had many paranormal abilities typical of an alien being. Things like premonition, healing power, telepathy to a certain extent. I was a great wizard. Moreover, ancient Egypt worshipped Orion, the three stars in the Orion belt, namely Mintaka, Alnitak and Alnilam. The three Great Pyramids of Giza were built in homage to these three stars. And the Orion belt is the seat of the Magnificent Reptilian Empire. This is more than just a coincidence. There was an intense connection between the ancient Egyptians and the reptilians.

Unfortunately, I only managed to see small bits of images, and I did not achieve clear perceptions of how that was done, their rituals or their connection to the reptilians. If only I could grasp a little of this knowledge, how nice. But that was not allowed. Nevertheless, I enjoyed very much these memories in particular.

The second experience was being an ancient Roman soldier in the beginning of the persecution of Christian's period that means some time after Nero. His name was Leptunius or Tertulius, I am not sure.He was a very brave soldier who killed many rebels in the Northern frontier of the Empire, and for doing so was awarded and allowed to retire. With his wages he managed to open a small brothel in Rome starting with three slave prostitutes. He died relatively old at the age of 45 years old in this way.

He agreed with the persecution of Christians which he considered the duty of a righteous Emperor. Like many others, he considered that the Christians were bad to the Empire, some kind of sabotage from a very unsubmissive province like Judea. Such ideas, he thought, could weaken brave Roman men. The idea of becoming a lamb or a fish meant accepting to be devoured. How could they identify themselves with that? The Egyptian gods existed there, too, but they were animals so full of strength, such as Lions, hawks, the ibis, the jackal. He thought: '-Who wants to be a prey?"Or "-Who worships a prey?"In short ,he supported these tortures.

This was very interesting to me, because I could see things from another perspective, their perspective, different from what we see nowadays. It looks horrible and nonsensical today, but it was justified by their beliefs back then. It made perfect sense to them. It was not just the act of some mad Emperor. They thought it was a very subversive cult, even though they tolerated many foreign religions with all kinds of odd beliefs.

It is hard to recall periods between two reincarnations, "the heaven" periods. It is much easier to access the material reincarnation periods, because they have stronger emotions and many traumas. Pain and strong emotions cause a serious imprint in the soul. That is why we should live intensively every moment of our passage on Earth, because many sensations can only be achieved with a physical body.

An unstable world like planet Earth provides lives with too many ups and downs, pleasure and pain, happiness and sorrow. Yet ,I have vague memories of spiritual guides talking to me prior to a reincarnation. These beings were primarily humans responsible for my passage on Earth. There were also aliens, but those were not allowed to interfere. Such interferences would harm the purity of the human experience. Every human being on Earth has spiritual guides of their own. Nobody is alone, although we sometimes feel forsaken. The guides match their protégés in nature, beliefs and personality

After my death as a Roman legionary, I had a talk with my spiritual guide. I wanted to live in the East, get to know oriental cultures. I was granted this opportunity. Therefore I was born at least twice in Old China. The first time I was a maid in a rich home in a small town. Though it was a very limited existence, it was pleasant in a way. I have beautiful memories of that life, and a peaceful sensation when I look at it. In comparison to a cruel Ancient Rome, Old China was a paradise.

The second existence in the East was like a Chinese scholar, a teacher. It was even better, because I had the opportunity to study the classics, something a woman, especially a poor woman could never do. I learned a lot from this one. Confucius, Buddha, the Chinese classics. Wonderful.

The next existence that I recall clearly was in 18th century France. I lived in the small town of Amiens, where there is a famous cathedral and where Jules Verne was born a century later. I was born a woman called Lucille. A middle class lady married to a cheese maker. She had two children she did not love at all. "-I made them to please my mother-in-law.' She says. She barely met them.A maid would take care of them. (In fact that was usual in those days, I discovered that in historic records).Those children were simply part of a marital arrangement. She was unfaithful, just like her husband. One of her hobbies was shouting at her maids, make them feel bad. However, I think I was lucky to have lived in such a beautiful historic period.

Lucille envied the aristocratic ladies of Paris, since she was just a provincial copy of their style. And for that, she would not hesitate to steal money earmarked for the children's education. She would steal it and buy clothes and jewelry for herself. She could not care less. She was also into trying little witchcrafts.

She was illiterate. Some years ago I studied French and my teacher was amazed how fast I was learning. But I could not write at all, there was a huge discrepancy between my written and my spoken French (in this present life).

She did not suffer serious consequences of the revolution, because she was not noble and she lived in a small town. She died of natural causes in the early days of the 19th century.

The hardest reincarnation I remember so far was in mid 19th century Brazil. I was a young black female slave working in the big farm house, a "mucama", as they called here in Brazil.I cooked and cleaned for the Portuguese farm owners. And the white master harassed me sexually. He raped me, usually in front of other slaves, one of his favorite kicks.

This is the nature of karma. One day you are master, another you are servant. One day you exploit, the other you are exploited. The seeds of regret could wait two or more lives before they bear their fruits.

The most recent life I remember was in the radio days, in Tunisia. I was a middle aged, fat, married Muslim woman. I was unloved, merely a servant for my husband. I carried bags with ingredients for the foods I would prepare and in special occasions, I would have the pleasure of buying some nice fabric. Going to the market, gossiping and shopping were my only moments of joy. In the market I heard the radio talking about the war, about Hitler and Mussolini. In short, a sad and boring existence.

The only reason why I am reporting these lives is to show that an extraterrial origin does not mean you are in any way special or different. People who are perfectly normal and even quite uninteresting might be a "starchild", a reincarnation of an alien being. They are not necessarily born privileged. My potential reptilian origin did not provide me a birth in a powerful, influential family. On the contrary, the reincarnation of an alien being might be born sick or weak, because his or her astral body does not fit the human form properly. If an alien is facing one of his or her first reincarnations on Earth, he will probably have health problems and adaptation problems. He tends to grow up lonely, with not so strong family ties. Socializing can also be very difficult for them.

Some UFO researchers call that condition a "starchild", the reincarnation of an alien being in a human form. They might be social misfits, lonely people, and unhappy people. Some are willing to commit suicide from an early age, even as children. Others are born sick, with inefficient organs, poor sight , bad digestion and so on. For that reason, some individuals who are perfectly ordinary might be constantly monitored by aliens who are aware of what they really are.

In Brazil, a book called "Banned from Capella"(Os exilados de Capela, by Armond, Edgard, Ed. Aliança,1987)achieved tremendous success with a similar story. In Brazil, the "Espirita" movement has been growing steadily over the years. Not only believing in reincarnation, they also believe that any soul can be reborn in another gender, nation, ethnic group or planet, depending on the circumstances.

"Banned from Capella" tells about the star system Capella, located in the Auriga constellation. This planet would have reached a higher level of evolution some 40,000 years ago. Nevertheless, some individuals could not keep up with it and they represented an obstacle to that new step of planetary evolution. Therefore a major catastrophe befell upon them, and exterminated part of the population in a kind of doomsday. The spirits of the ones who failed in adapting to the newly evolved world were sent to primitive planet Earth. Here they started again as cavemen. Not only that, although they were imperfect, they brought along a reminiscent memory of their planet of origin. For that reason, they were specially intelligent and gifted in comparison to the already existing cavemen. Their arrival has sped up human evolution on Earth as a consequence. In comparison to the original cavemen, those "starchildren from Capella", were smarter, kinder and better organized.

According to this book, everyone today is also a starchild. Everyone would be the reincarnation of a being from the Capella star. This may be true. But the other kind of starchild

I mention here is the more recent one, the one who came here later from somewhere else. This recent starchild has adaptation issues and he or she suffers in a way. Probably, this person is being monitored by their original alien race, whatever that is. They come from different origins, different planets and they fit in Earth's life form in different degrees. In some cases, alien doctors intervene early on, in order to keep this human body functioning. This also explains many abduction cases, involving medical "repair", as they call it.

WHY SO MUCH AVERSION TO REPTILIANS?

The very first reported case of a reptilian being dates back to 1967, in Ashland, Nebraska. Police officer Herbert Schirmer said he had been abducted by reptile-looking alien beings. He had been taken into an oval-shaped spacecraft that he had mistaken for a truck on the road. The case was investigated by UFO researcher and psychologist Dr. Leo Sprinkle. Herbert described the creatures as non-violent and even friendly. They claimed they had their bases on planet Venus and they did not deny the fact that they stole electrical energy from human power sources. Nothing in that case justifies all the fear and aversion that was later associated to those beings.

In more recent years, these beingshave been demonized. This process is based essentially on the association with the Biblical serpent that tempted Eve, as in Genesis 3:1-5 and other mythical or religious passages, such as the Aztec god

Quetzalcoatl or the Hindu Nagas. In short, they were associated to Satan due to their appearance.

British author David Icke specialized in the reptilian issue. He speaks very negatively about them, with a constant association between reptilian and the Illuminati society.TV series such as "V the final Battle" (1984) helped to stimulate the concept of reptilians as demons and cannibals. Therefore, reptilians and reptiles alike are seen as evil by nature, anti-human beings.

Reptilians are intelligent beings that evolved from something like a small dinosaur instead of a mammal. This could have happened on Earth easily if dinosaurs had not gone extinct. Dr. Dale Russell, paleontologist from the Ottawa National Museum in Canada declared that the Troodon, a small, bird-like dinosaur could have evolved into intelligent life.

Similarly, there are insect-like beings, beings that look like a praying mantis.These, too evolved from a different class of animals, the insects, which is possible. Not only mammals have the potential for developing intelligence.Of course, by evolving from an insect or a reptile, these beings think and feel quite differently from a human. They created societies with totally different rules and values. It is not hard to imagine that reptiles are less prone to affection than mammal-based evolution beings. Probably more hierarchical and less compassionate than soft hearted humans (although I do not see many around).Not paternalistic, they would value competence and force. But that alone does not turn them into demons. They would not visit Earth just to relish its destruction or to displease God. If the do business with unethical human groups that is because humans also tend to do selfish things.

Negotiating with primitive planets such as Earth infringes frontally the commandments of the Confederation of Planets. The Confederation of Planets sees worlds like Earth like a fruit that must ripe by itself, like an egg that should be left alone to hatch. Trying to help or negotiate with planets like Earth represents an irreversible interference,the end of their innocence.

What reptilians want does not differ much from what rich countries on Earth do to poor countries. They are willing to exchange technology for raw materials and expand their influence through commerce. But the Confederation of Planets considers this a terrible form of dependence. In other words, alien species have different points of view concerning how a planet like Earth should be handled.

Alien species are in contact with each other and they are fully aware of each other's agenda. They see each other in mother ships and they meet openly. They disagree in many aspects but they do not often fight because of that. So, it is not as simple as "good ' on one side and "evil' on the other side. It is much more complex than that. Non-interference, for instance might be very frustrating to humans who are craving for full contact and quick evolution. They will have to wait thousands of years to be able to contact other species in an equal level. If mankind survives that long.

In his research on reptilians, David Icke met South African sangoma (a priest) Credo Mutwa, in his documentary "The Reptilian Agenda" (UFO TV, 2004). In his experience, Credo was taken by gray aliens who reported to reptilians. Credo's tribal traditions described reptilians that he called the "Chitauri',whose terrible appearance he compared to Star Wars' Darth Maul (a demon-looking character).During this interview, Credo also comments that the Chitauri still have an underground settlement in the Matopo mountains of Zimbabwe.

The most relevant part here is Credo's comments on the mythical arrival of the Chitauri. According to him, this took place thousands of years ago, in a time when humans led a very idyllic existence. The Chitauri had promised fantastic things to these innocent humans if they agreed to work in the mines for them. This is especially the case in South Africa, because of the abundance of gold and many other riches. As a matter of fact, the Chitauri would have betrayed them by removing the natural human telepathic ability that existed previously. They substituted that for the spoken language, so that lying and hiding thoughts would be easier. The Chitauri would also have divided mankind in two sexes, something that did not exist prior to them, according to Credo. The Chitauri queen felt sorry for these poor humans and tried to help them. By doing so, she infuriated the Chitauri king Mobaba Samohongo, who would have beheaded her.

Despite of its fascinating details, it is incredible that such antipathy towards reptilians would have grown so easily among the public in general, based on just a few documentaries. The very idea of reptiles as malignant seems to be naturally accepted as common sense by people in general. It is hard for them to imagine otherwise. After that, every evil thing on Earth, especially war, exploitation, pollution as well as the Illuminati and their allegedly nasty deeds were permanently associated to the reptilians.Such ideas are promptly accepted, because reptiles in general look nasty.

By the way, very little is known about the Illuminatis' real intentions. There is lot of hearsay about them, and too little confirmation. This secret society really exists; it was founded by Adam Weishaupt in 18th century Bavaria, visibly inspired by philosophers such as Rousseau. But a secret society is secret, and it is hard to know more about them. Who really has access to this kind of information? Who knows what they really do?

People who advocate the idea of reptilians as the source of all mankind's suffering are very unilateral. They underestimate human ability to do evil. They have this patronizing attitude towards mankind which is seen as vulnerable and easily misled. This idea is condescending. It is almost like believing that tribal or primitive people are incapable of doing nasty things. These people replace the old belief in demons for a more contemporary one, a belief in the evil, manipulative reptilian who misleads mankind.

Sincerely speaking, I am not sure if all those images where I saw myself as a reptilian in a previous live are real. Sometimes I think suspect they could be an artifice in order to make me see them as friends or even family. This would be the best way to break any resistance on my side, so that I would welcome them with open arms. This would take advantage of my sense of no belonging and my strong attraction towards UFO research.

On the other hand, If it is really so, I mean, If I really am the reincarnation of a reptilian being, I gladly accept that. I have no shame of that despite of their bad reputation in the UFO research scene. I am what I am. To each being its own. Animals like lions, scorpions, alligators, and snakes live on Earth and they are neither evil nor good. They simply exist and do according to their nature. Who should we blame for the nasty things they do? If nature consisted exclusively of flowers and rabbits, there would no killing in the forest. But that is not the way it is.

Besides, mankind has not been delighting the universe with their kind deeds, either. Are they?

MENTAL CONTACT IS LESS DISTURBING THAN A PHYSICAL ABDUCTION

I realized that over time, as mental contact evolves, physical abduction tends to become less frequent. This is not the case for people who are being used in a hybrid reproduction program. But is so for the ones who merely have a mental contact with alien species for any reason.

For those who have a more mental kind of contact, actual abductions are partially replaced by astral projections. I would call them "astral abductions". That means, visiting alien bases, entering spaceships and learning from them through some kind of long distance transmission.

That is why gray aliens got their bad reputation. They are exactly the ones who perform the more physical kind of abduction. They prepare human individuals for a deeper contact, by placing implants, medical procedures and things like that. They do the dirty job.

Later in the alien–human contact process, the same "evil" grays will be seen hand-in-hand with benevolent Nordic aliens or scary reptilians or any other species, inside a mother ship. This is constantly reported, abductees, or contactees (if there is any difference) are amazed when they realize that all species coexist in the same ships. That means different alien species working together in a common project, or using the same transportation. Many people think that there are good guys and bad guys in opposite sides, but, at the end, there is just a big community of aliens in space. They all meet, talk, and travel together.

Gray aliens are not good at talking, so experiences with them tend to be boring, scary and you do not learn much from them. Mental contact comes later, when other species appear on the scene. The gray alien abduction sometimes is more like a preparatory level for something else. Gray alien abductions only continue forever if there is a reproductive program involved. Otherwise they will be replaced by less traumatic forms of contact.

That is my case. I do not have good genes as they told me, a good genetic constitution, which means I can not produce healthy hybrid babies. Therefore gray alien abductions became infrequent in my case. A more mental, psychic kind of contact replaced it to a certain extent.

Such mental contacts are unreliable. We never know for sure where the "I" ends and the "They" starts. There is lot of personal interpretation in those messages. These messages are pretty much like a long distance course by mail. You receive the information but there is nobody to explain it or to comment it to you. That explains the tremendous differences among contactee's ideas worldwide. This is a very uncertain method where the message goes through the interpretive mind of a human being.

However, if we trust exclusively in "scientific" UFO research, we will have little or no understanding of this phenomenon, we reach a dead end. Contactees and their messages are imperfect, but they give us a clue of what is going on, they provide another piece in this puzzle. This is the alien way of gradually disclosing the reality of their presence without shaking this world too much. The truth about aliens is a slow, painstaking discovery.It starts with few individuals in different places, and not in total agreement with one another.

PART 2 OTHER REPORTS

OTHER PEOPLE AND THEIR REPORTS

The people mentioned in this part are connected personally to me in many ways. Some are just acquaintances, others friends and others are members of my UFO vigil group.

Some of their stories are so weird that I hesitated to publish them. But I trust their honesty and I think they add more important facts to our quest for understanding the aliens. We should not prematurely judge them with preconceived notions of what is "normal" and what is "not normal" in an alien contact. There is no such a thing.

ROMULO'S REPORT: A PSYCHIC

Romulo (pseudonym) is a 37 year old man who lives in Sao Paulo and works in an advertising agency. He belongs to a "Espirita' group, a Brazilian spiritualist movement that believes in reincarnation and charity. These people develop psychic abilities in specific courses, and expertise in energetic healing and communication with the dead. He is also very fond of Hindu and Eastern spirituality. As far as Romulo is concerned, UFO research and aliens are dangerous and scary topics. Yet, he kept asking me about it, out of sheer curiosity.

Romulo is a great clairvoyant; he sees deceased people and many other manifestations. He dedicates his gift to helping people in need in the spiritualist group he belongs to. He does that regularly.He does that totally for free,he never profits from it.

In one of his visits to Angra dos Reis (Rio de Janeiro state) he saw a UFO hovering above the sea. "It looked like a music CD, it shifted colors all the time", he said. His mother witnessed it too. There is a nuclear power station there and he thought they were investigating it. However, he requested mentally that they leave. "-I did not want any business with them." he said. Apparently, they left peacefully.

In fact, they did not give up on him. Two years later, he had a visitor in his bedroom. It was 3 a.m. and he woke up with an unpleasant odor, just like the smell of a swamp full of decomposed vegetable matter. And he could see a light portal opening and a small white creature came out of it. The creature was in every way similar to a gray alien with big black eyes, skinny and apparently naked with no visible genitals.Romulo compared the being's color to white marshmallow.The being was levitating one foot above ground ,and he spoke telepathically to Romulo. Romulo did not get frightened, because he had seen so many spirits before, some of them very ugly or threatening, so no big deal about that.

The being asked: "-Why do you keep asking about us to the one who has contact? Would you like to have a contact of your own? Come and meet us."

Romulo turned down the offer straight away. He said he was not interested, and asked the being to leave immediately. The being insisted and showed images of a small town through the portal. He said it was Pirassununga, a military base town 200 miles far from Sao Paulo. He said: "-Meet us somewhere near that place, we will be there."

Once again, Romulo turned down the offer and the being left using the same portal. When he finally managed to sleep again, much time later, he heard the cell phone ringing. The area code was 019.The next day he called this number to see who called. It was a lady, and she did not remember having called anyone that night, especially not him. But he dared asking where she was. And, as you can imagine, it was a call from Pirassununga!

Afterwards, every Wednesday night, around 3 a.m., the light portal would appear and oftentimes the little being came out of it. Romulo repelled the being repeatedly until the visits stopped altogether.

Romulo was upset and he talked to me. He threw away pictures I gave him, pictures taken during my vigils. He knew the entity did not visit him under my request, but he began to avoid me a little. I replied by saying I would gladly fill in for him in such an encounter. I told him to offer the being my name as a substitute, and I would go for sure. But it seems I was not invited. That made me jealous again. However, I enjoyed when the being said: "-The one who has contact."

That demonstrates how contagious alien contact may be. Contactees or abductees have implants. Those implants act like cameras transmitting images and sound to some alien spacecraft. They can track down an individual through this implant and see who is around that person and doing what. In so doing, they may find others who are also interesting for them.

The most surprising thing for me is that the being allowed Romulo a choice. They usually take people against their will. He was privileged. Contact does not always happen to the ones who crave for it, they usually happen against one's will. Many people resist and try to fight abduction with no success.

For the same reason it sounds incredible to me when I hear reports of UFO contact groups who make appointments with aliens successfully. They receive a telepathic message and go to the appointed place. Unfortunately that has never happened to me. I am not saying it is impossible, it is just not that way for me or anybody I know.

MR. MANGA: PURE IN THE HEART

Mr. Manga is a country man. "Manga" refers to a Brazilian breed of horse, the "mangalarga'.Therefore, he was horse rider. But due to health problems, he was obliged to retire.Nowadays he lives in Piracicaba, in Sao Paulo state. He belongs to Isis's UFO vigil group.

In his homeland, Mato Grosso state, he used to stay out at night, hunting in the forest. Many times he had witnessed strange lights moving in the woods, but never really tried to explain what it was. Seeing those lights was quite usual for country people in Brazil and they did not call them UFOs or whatever, they thought they were spirits or unexplainable natural phenomena. They call it "Mãe-do-ouro" ("mother of gold"), a nature spirit who guards goldmines. They believe there is gold wherever those things are seen. The lights would represent a warning to stay away from it, according to their beliefs.

Manga is not an uncultured man. He reads a lot and he is eager to learn. Nowadays he discusses UFO related topics based on texts in Portuguese or English with great logic and lucidity.

One night in 2008 he woke up and noticed that three gray aliens were in his bedroom. They had those big black eyes, the ash gray skin and the skinny body, everything that characterizes those beings. One of them was holding a tube he thought it was a gun. They were walking around the room and investigating objects in it. They behaved as if they were not interested in Manga and his wife. His wife was in deep sleep and nothing would wake her up.

I asked him if he did not get scared. He said: "-Why would I? They were being cool."He simply let them do their thing while he watched.

Unfortunately, there was a Rottweiler in the room, and it began to roar. The dog saw the grays as a threat and it was about to attack them. Then the one with the tube aimed it at the dog and shot the animal with some kind of laser beam. The dog fell asleep immediately.

Manga felt uncontrollably sleepy in a few minutes, something that is frequently reported during abductions and bedroom visits. He could no longer keep his eyes open.I can barely believe they were there just to admire the room. The actual procedure probably started when he fell asleep.

Sadly enough, the dog developed a spongy cancer in its mouth in the exact spot where it was shot. The dog died in less than a month. The veterinarian said Rottweilers are prone to cancer and gave little attention to it. It is incredible that Mr. Manga does not hate the beings for that. He understands that they did it out of self defense. He is not at all resentful, he forgave them completely.

Mr Manga's sister had an experience too. She was healed by aliens. She suffered form a grave case of throat cancer and doctors told she would not live long. One night she was visited by insect-looking beings that were in every way similar to a praying mantis. She was not completely awake, but she saw them injecting some kind of iodine in her throat and she was miraculously cured in a few days.

Although she has never been submitted to hypnosis, her story is very relevant. Many people tend to think that "ugly" beings are hostile, and they are willing to meet a human-looking being only. This is a big mistake. We should not prejudge an alien by its appearance, as we can see in the case of such benevolent beings who saved her life.

HANS' CASE: "NORDICS" AREN'T ALWAYS THAT NICE

This is the case of Mr. Hans, a man of European origin who lives in Sao Paulo, Brazil, married, business administrator, 64 years old. A typical European man who does not care for spiritualism, a materialistic man.

Mr. Hans's story sounds more like an astral projection than an actual abduction to me. It is a very rich story. One night in 2010, he saw himself in the outside of the house. He was surrounded by strangers. As soon as he saw them, he felt "strong and mighty". There was a man there, he shook his hand and the man complained, he said Hans was grabbing his hand too strong. He hugged a girl, and she said the same. She felt suffocated by his embrace.

Since Mr. Hans felt that herculean power, he jumped and stood up on the top of his house roof. He felt like a superman, a weightless being. He began to admire the beautiful night sky. Then he saw a circular formation of five rectangular objects coming down right above him. They were shinny, with a beautiful bluish light that did not hurt the eyes, like moonlight. These rectangular UFOs had soft, curvy edges.

He knew it was too late to run, but he had a comfortable feeling about it.He was not willing to resist.A beam of light came down from these objects and he describes it as "a carpet of light" which took him gently into the ship. This beam of light did that in seconds. As soon as he got in, he looked around and saw a squeaky clean white room with key panels, apparently not very complicated ones.

He had a feeling he was being observed although there was nobody there.he felt some kind of strange invisible presence there. He tried to talk to it, but there was no reply.He could sense the movements of the spaceship.They were smooth, like an elevator.There was no need for seatbelts.At a point, the ship landed and he could get off.

Out there, he saw a beautiful field with grass and trees.But they looked unnatural, pretty much as if they had been arranged artificially.There were white houses here and there, and he describes them as "simple and decent".There were lots of people walking around.They were all blond, with a blank look in their eyes.They were all wearing kung fu-like suits in light green with a white symbol on the right. He does not remember how this symbol looked like.

If Mr.Hans tried to talk to them, they were always evasive.They walked away from him.Only one of them answered laconically: "-So, you are among the ones who were brought here today." And that was it. "-A completely useless comment", Mr Hans said.

He wandered for a while, and he finally entered one of those white houses.There was a couch in the back of the room, and three of those beautiful blondes were sitting there.Two were seated in a normal position,but one of them had her legs straddled, looking as if she was waiting for sexual intercourse. He promptly accepted that and invited her to go somewhere and do it.He thought she was wonderful.

Without a word, the blond girl grabbed his hand and took him to a garden with a perfectly circular lake right in the middle. At the entrance of that area, there was a table with a kind of receptionist who also ignored him completely.There were more of those white houses circling around this lake. He understood that it was a kind of sex club, and he was expecting a very exciting experience.

 The girl conducted him to one of those houses.She pushed him into a room, locked him up in the dark room and left him all alone.He waited and waited and nobody showed up anymore.That was the end of the experience.

He woke up the next day feeling incredibly strong and energized.He had a pleasant feeling, even though he was frustrated about not having finished his sexual intercourse with that blond girl.

After that experience, something changed in Mr. Hans' life. He became less concerned about mundane problems. Those things seemed less relevant now.He realized that so many things we consider important in this world are totally irrelevant, and he felt amazingly free.

This sensation is commonly reported among alien contact experiencers.They feel detached from material things, traditions, rules or even religious beliefs. They sense a blissful indifference; a nirvana-like feeling of supreme inner peace.That is the consequence of such a cosmic experience.For many experiencers, there is a period where it gets difficult to bear the normal routine of their lives. They no longer feel interested in their jobs, family or friends.They see those things as obstacles to the liberation of their souls.

For that reason, aliens avoid too intensive contact process with humans. Otherwise, contactees will lose interest in earthly things and might eventually commit suicide.I believe that the members of Heaven's Gate and other similar cases were victims of an extremely incorrect contact proccess.They were not crazy, as we can imagine from the outside, they were just conducted improperly by real aliens.Some aliens promise humans that if they commit suicide, they will be free to reincarnate in a better world.This is one of the dangers of alien contact. But usually, contact happens more gradually. The exposure to aliens and their beautiful worlds leads humans to inconformity, but that fades away as time goes by. In this case, the contactee himself will realize that he is not going to live anywhere else in this existence and ends up accepting it.

The relationship between alien contact and sexuality is a well-known one.Both Christian and Muslim medieval literature are full of stories of non-human beings who seduce humans.The medieval Christian incubus sucubus was believed to appear in the night to have sexual intercourse with humans.Muslim scholars associate aliens to the "Al-Jinn", the geniuses that are mentioned in the Koran.Geniuses could be faithful or unfaithful to Allah, and they craved sexual intercourse with humans.They also interfered with human beings in many other ways.The Koran explains that Jinns(geniuses) are 'smokeless fire". These beings are capable of invisibility whenever they feel like. According to Koran, they would be predominantly mischievous. There are many references to them in Arabic literature, especially in Al-Rumi (1207-1273 a.D.) who claimed to be in direct contact with them.These jinns told Al-Rumi the basics about the solar system, atomic structure and human reproduction right in the middle ages.They told him the Earth moved around the Sun, not the opposite.They told him about the sperm cell fusing with the ovum in the womb and the atomic structure we know today, with electrons spinning around the nucleus.In those days, his ideas were seen as pure poetry.

British occultist Aleister Crowley (1875-1947) also had an encounter with a being that identified itself as "Lam". This took place in the "Amalantrah" rituals he performed in 1918 in New York City.The being's head was in every way similar to a modern gray alien's head.Aleister Crowley compared its head to an egg. Aleister's followers nowadays associate Lam to a kind of egg-shaped astral projection capsule capable of going to remote areas of the universe.All that happened in a time when there was no talk of UFO research and gray aliens.

UFO researchers in general tend to think that human sexual intercourse with aliens is for reproductive purposes only.They would be part of a selective reproduction program, aiming at generating hybrids or some kind of eugenics.In Brazil alone, a farmer called Antonio Villas Boas was abducted in 1957 and obliged to have sexual intercourse with a short, blond,human-looking female alien.As soon as the copulation finished, she pointed at the sky,and that meant the baby yet to be born would live in another planet.That was the first time such an event had been mentioned, at least in Brazil.Many others occurred later.

American UFO researchers place great importance to this reproductive program.Dr. David Jacobs' book "The Threat"demonstrate how women are forced to participate in human-alien hybridization programs conducted by gray aliens.Other authors like Whtley Strieber and Budd Hopkins say basically the same.

However, there are cases of aliens interacting with humans in a more seductive way.In the 1970's Brazil, contactee M. Bianca told about her abduction case and the beautiful extraterrial being called Karran.He was tall, handsome and he had black hair and black slanted eyes, like an Asian man,a very attractive being according to her..

Similarly, in Mr Hans', case as well as in my own case, "Nordic" aliens appear naked or in sexy positions.They seem to be aware of the effect this may cause.Even if they are not particularly interested in real sexual intercourse,they apparently take advantage of that. That breaks the abductee's resistance and ensures more cooperation.Or maybe that helps in making the abductee yearn for another experience as soon as possible.Sexuality would be a bait to attract humans.They can easily read our thoughts.Therefore they know our sexual preference and taste and use that as a teaser.

Mr Hans has demonstrated a high level of paranormal powers over the years, despite of his skeptcism.Later he told me about other amazing experiences he had.He experienced many events of astral projection where he could fly and feel exceptionally strong.

He also had seen UFOs prior to the "Nordic alien" experience he had. In 1972, for instance, he was at beach with a girlfriend at night and they were about to have sex. Suddenly a disc-shaped UFO appeared above the sea. The girl pointed at the object which stood still over the sea. Hans ran to the house where they were staying, looking for a pair of binoculars he had.As soon as he left, the object flew away in a straight line and never came back.

In 1969, Hans lived in a big house in Sao Paulo, close to the Ibirapuera park.One night, he had the scariest experience of his entire life.He went to bed that night with an unpleasant gut feeling. Later that night he felt a powerful presence in his bedroom. The thing looked like a huge amoeba ready to involve his body completely.Firstly he saw the entity outside the house, through the window.Then the thing crossed the window easily. He was overwhelmed with utmost horror.He felt its negativity.The thing drained his vital force completely.

He tried to hit the wall, because he could not scream.The wall made no sound whatsoever.The electric light from a lamp grew dim, he was feeling weaker and weaker.He could do nothing but pray.After a while, the thing went away by itself. It dissipated as it crossed the window again.The lights got back to normal, and he saw that his hands were bleeding and the wall was tainted with his blood.Mr. Hans strongly believes he met the devil or the worst kind of vampire imaginable.

I am sure that Mr. Hans' experiences will go on, no matter how skeptical he is. And as for him, all he really wants is to meet that beautiful alien blonde again to solve some unfinished business.

ICARUS' CASE: INCUBUS SUCUBUS?

Icarus is a pseudonym I chose for a 35 year old man who lives in Sao Paulo.He works as a musician and he hates UFO related topics for a good reason.Yet, he had the courage to tell me some of his most horrible memories ever.

As a teenager he had nightly experiences with aliens that started when he was only 14 years old. One night he saw a small group of gray aliens coming from behind his bedroom door.They were so skinny that 4 or 5 aliens fitted perfectly behind that normal door.They jumped at him, grabbed him and paralysed him.After that, they performed a whole string of unpleasant medical exams.

This happened many times, repeatedly, over his teenage years.Sometimes he was taken inside the spaceship in a beam of light.In such occasions, he felt suffocated, and he could not breathe. Only his mind was still active, his body was completely immobilized.Inside the UFO, he could only see an extremely bright light and a surgery table where the gray aliens performed more exams.This went on until he was 17 years old, and then they suddenly stopped.

This is a classical gray alien abduction case except for one thing.A very traumatic detail he has never forgotten in his entire life.

In some of those abductions, after they finished their job, those gray aliens would bring someone else. It was a demon or a faun-looking being with a full erection. This being would grab the kid from behind and rape him.The gray aliens helped the faun-looking being in doing so. It seemed like they wanted to bring fear and horror to its highest levels.

No matter how hard I try to understand the reasons for this, I do not really get to a conclusion. This is certainly not a selective reproduction program. And it is not one of those cases of "alien seduction", either.So, how can we interpret this?

My first hypothesis is that such a beast-like humanoid would have sexual needs of his own.In this case; the gray aliens were satisfying those needs accordingly.If so, I have never heard of anything like this before.

The second possibility is hallucination caused by extreme fear. Possibly, he was introduced painful mechanical instruments in his anus. Icarus might have had nightmarish hallucinations because of it. His fear would lead him to sheer insanity and he would no longer distinguish fantasy from reality. Fear could generate such demonic figures.

The third hypothesis is the one I support the most. I tend to believe that the devilish creature was real. It could be used for imposing discipline,therefore representing some form of punishment. If Icarus disobeyed the aliens too much, they might have opted for such a terrible course of action.That explains why this always happened at the end of the abduction event. If some aliens choose seduction as a way to gain cooperation, others prefer fear.However, it is very unusual.

Each spaceship is commanded by a different capitain. Depending on the capitain and the crew's disposition, they might be more or less violent, gentle, communicative, respectful and so on. One can not expect standard behaviors coming from aliens.They are unpredictable and that is the most dangerous aspect of alien abduction.Therefore, I do not think this report is absurd at all, and I totally endorse it.

JACOB'S CASE: "BECAUSE YOU ARE REALLY SPECIAL"

The case I am about to tell you came from a 25-year old man who studies International law at the university. I will call him Jacob, although that is not his real name, in order to protect his identity.He is of Jewish origin and a very bright student.He is deeply interested in Judaism and studying cultures in general.

Early on, Jacob had some paranormal abilities. When he was five years old, his grandmother died.At the same time as she died in another town, he saw her in his bedroom.She waved goodbye to him and left.

That was not the only time he sensed spiritual presences. Apparently he is also capable of moving objects with his mind. This happened in a few occasions.He could move small object by staring at them.

More recently he started having some odd sensations.One night he was taken inside a UFO, although he has no idea of how that was done.The place was squeaky clean and totally white. A very immaculate, circular room.As soon as he arrived, he was received by a gray alien who invited him telepathically to visit their facilties.

The first thing they showed him was a nursery.This one too was immaculate and all in white. There were many cradles with newborn babies in them.All these babies were alien-human hybrids.He asked the alien why he was showing him that. The alien being sounded exhilarated when he said:

"-Look, they are **all** yours! That is because you are special."

Jacob was startled; he said nothing.He did not remember any sexual intercourse with an alien. He did not recall any abductions, either.How could they possibly collect his sperm without him seeing it? Somehow they did it. He was happy to hear that, anyhow.He enjoyed the idea.

His experience ended at that point, he has no further recollections of that event.In another occasion, he was taken again to a spaceship. He is not sure if this is some sort of astral projection or a real abduction.He has not undergone hypnosis regression therapy so far.In this second experience, he met a clone of himself.The clone was wearing a suit, and he was slightly different from the real Jacob. Small imperfections of skin, or the fact that he is a little overwight were not present in that clone.The clone smiled at him and said hallo.

In another oocasion, Jacob saw himself inside a UFO which was landed in a forest. From a window, he could see the triangular court where this and many other similar spaceships were parked.Inside that ships, there were many other human beings. They were all asking themselves what they were doing there. On the outside, gray aliens were observing the ships with those humans inside.Suddenly he heard an announcement that the ships should return the humans to their homes in strict order of arrival.This announcement came from a flying metallic ball, because the grays, as we know, are telepathic. They do not speak.

Butfor some reason they decided to let humans know what was going on.This time they decided to communicate through traditional human methods. And for that, they need vocal or written messages coming from machines.After that, they departed and the experience ends in that point.

The fact that Jacob is a Jew has some relevance.Would that be the reason why he was "so special"? In this case, his genetic lineage could have been followed up for centuries, even thousands of years by the aliens.Many authors claim that passages of the Bible are UFO encounters.Starting from Erich Von Daniken in the late 1960's,many authors said that. Ezekiel's visions and Moses' seeing a flying roll while crossing the desert could easily be interpreted as UFO encounters.The same goes for Elijah's ascension to heaven. Israelian UFO researcher Barry Chamish also comments in his book "Return of the Giants" that giant aliens would have returned to modern Israel.These tall creatures would be similar to the giants described in the Old Testament.According to him, this would be a typically Israelian alien appearance that is not usual anywhere else. It is hard to determine statistically whether Jews are more prone to abductions than anybody else or not. But I met two other people of Jewish origin who had relevant encounters with aliens.Maybe the Nephilim giants are really more than a mith. And some angels could also be an ancient interpretation for the alien presence. But this subject is more for UFO archeologists and authors like

Daniken or J.J.Benitez. I am more into the direct experience with aliens.

KARREL'S CASE: FERTILITY

Antonio Karrel, 31 years old lives in Piracicaba with his parents. He works for a local newspaper. He is a rather jovial man who laughs a lot. He tells jokes all the time, and he likes bragging about the size of his penis and his sexual performance.This is something Brazilian many men like to do. He does not correspond to the image I had of a contactee who is highly spiritualized and introspective.Not at all.He is extroverted and fun-loving.But the aliens chose him.

Karrel wakes up before dawn to work in the local newspaper.One of these days back in 2006, he left home at 5a.m. and the sky was still pitch-dark outside.He used to ride his motorcycle to get to work.When he turned right at the first corner on his way to work, he saw a huge disc hovering above the street, right in front of him. It should be some 30 feet above the ground level only. It was very low indeed.He stopped and began looking at it. He was fascinated.He was not afraid at all, because he had never heard of these terrible gray alien abductions that are so famous in the USA nowadays.

The UFO had a large, rectangular window. Through this window, Karrel could see two gray aliens staring at him.He also noticed the immaculate white color of its interior. One of those gray aliens was staring right at him, and communicating telepathically this way.In a split second, Karrel learned a million things through the alien's eyes.Just by looking at those eyes, he understood the purpose of that encounter and the internal distribution of the spaceship.He knew that ship was specialized in receiving humans, and there was a "human receiving sector' where human beings were secluded.This "download" of information was too strong for him, and little by little he is recovering the information as time goes by.

Incredible as it sounds, Karrel has no recollection of entering the UFO.This memory was probably erased from his brain.It is hard to imagine that aliens would fly low for an encounter just to say hallo and leave.Something else happened that day.

After that, he had a string of weird sensations. He started dreaming of aliens and UFOs very often. He could sense a strange presence in his bedroom at night. He learned to deal with it, he says he likes it.He had confusing flashes of memory coming up at any moment.For this reason he joined the UFO vigil group, wishing to understand what was going on.What is more,he wanted to intensify his abductions! He wanted to repeat that experience more often.That is very unusual, most abductees fear or even hate their experiences.Sometimes they also fear and hate the ones who deal with that.But Karrel wants to go deeper and deeper into it.

No attempts of hypnosis therapy worked out well for him. When hypnotized, he says something similar to what he already knows.His complete experience was strongly locked up by the aliens. At a certain point, he always repeats the same words: "-The eyes, the eyes."(The alien's big black eyes).He remembers three gray aliens standing really close to him, with their faces almost rubbing his.One is staring close on the left side of his face, the other is on the right side of his face, and the strongest being with his eyes almost touching Karrel's eyes.

This highly hypnotic presence reinforced the command to forget what he saw.The alien's intimidating presence erased his memory completely.But in another hypnosis session he remembered that the spaceship that was hovering above the houses moved towards him and took him inside. That is obvious, but until that moment he did not know that.

Karrel is still a UFO research buff.He goes to UFO vigils whenever he can and shows a very positive attitude towards his abductions.He makes jokes about them too,and he summons the aliens to come back.I believe he is really managing to overcome his fears. He is even getting a little impatient, because they are taking too long to return.Although he does not know what happened to him clearly, he knows he probably has hybrid babies somewhere. After all, he believes the sexual potency and fertility he has will be of use for the aliens.And he likes this idea.

HEBE, MY MOTHER

My mother's name is Hebe. She is now 83 years old and she lives in Sao Paulo in a calm and quite uneventful old age.

Back in 1992, I decided to live in the Netherlands and I left her all alone.Worst of all, I am the only child.I was so eager to live in Europe that I forgot everything else.And so I went, and I stayed there for six years as an immigrant.I really miss that period of my life. I enjoyed it a lot.But that was not so funny for her.

Over the years, she grew bitter, and by the fifth year of my staying in Amsterdam, she had a serious heart attack.Her doctor called me to inform that she would not survive to it. I was deperated and I began to regret my choice.I wanted to reverse time and undo what I did. I hoped for a seconde chance.I felt hollow inside.The doctor even said I should not bother leaving Europe in a hurry, because I would not meet her still alive.

But that night she had some special visitors. She was in the Intensive Care unit of the hospital.The nurse was in deep sleep, it was about 3 a.m. A white screen separated the patients, and four beings came out from behind it.They were pale human-looking alien beings with pointed ears and slanted eyes.For this reason, I would consider her experience unusual, because this type is not commmnly reported. There are many kinds of aliens rather than just grays, reptilians and Nordics, but we got used to those as the most frequent ones.

They came closer to her and they carried many instruments.My mother thought it was unbelievable that the nurse and the other patients did not wake up. Suddenly she realized the emergency room became round in shape. In fact, she was no longer in the emergency room.Probably that was just some kind of holographic projection.One of the beings said telepathically:

"-It is about time that you come with us.'

She understood that he meant death, and they would somehow help her to die.In Brazil, people believe that a friendly spirit helps us to die when the time to die is come.And these aliens were the friendly spirits, thus.And she replied:

"-Not yet, please.Let me see my son one more time"

The alien being answered: "-In this case, you must be repaired.Close your eyes."

She did accordingly, and she felt a pressure in her chest.And then she slept deeply, as if she was sedated. The next day she got better and better and her heart healed miraculously.When I got the news, I called her and said that I would leave the Netherlands soon, just to spend some time with her in Brazil.This was my part of the healing process.

Some months later, I finally did what I promised.The first thing she told me when I arrived was her miraculous encounter with aliens and how wonderful they were.When I saw how lonely she had become, I realized I had to stay in Brazil. I knew the aliens did not "repair' her for just a quick visit on my side.I was supposed to stay closer to her. I simply knew it. I could no longer live with the remorse of leaving her behind to die alone while I was abroad. So I decided to stay, and I am still here in this country until today.With absolutely no regrets.

Concerning the aliens, reptilians, grays, Nordics and the others,if they are biological beings, there is good and bad in them. Neither demons nor angels, they are fallible creatures just like you.Do not demonize nor worship them. See them as older brothers who know more than you do.Only that.

I still wonder if I really am the reincarnation of a reptilian.Deep in my heart, it feels true.I believe they are a little rowdy, greedy and temperamental.And so am I.

My aunt Yara (the one who appeared to me in spirit) said once: "-You are a very nasty kid.You did not take your temperament after this family...We are good people."I guess she was right about that.I was born different from all my other relatives.

I do not think my mother is the reincarnation of a hotheaded reptilian like me.She has always been calm and submissive.Neither my father Jose, who was a calm and unselfish man. They are exactly the opposite of what I am.But maybe she is also of extraterrial origin. I suppose she belongs to the people who healed her in the hospital.Maybe.

Nevertheless, I am learning to live with such other beings, so different from me. I guess am becoming a more human kind of reptilian.

ABOUT THE AUTHOR

Chico Penteado, 44 years old, Brazilian, works as a teacher in a language institute.He lives in Sao Paulo, Sao Paulo state, Brazil.He dedicated his youth to spiritualistic studies, especially Buddhism and Afro-Brazilian Candomble.

Later in his life, he dedicated himself to UFO research.The focus of his interest is the direct UFO vigil, instead of academic study. He joined a UFO vigil group in 2002,and has been doing that ever since.He sees himself as an autonomous researcher and believes that practical experience is irreplaceable.

In this present work, he explains how his UFO vigil experience led him to direct contact with aliens and finally to a revelation.The revelation of his reptilian spiritual origin.

The book also contains reports from other individuals whose stories deserve special attention.These appear in part 2 of the book.

Chico Penteado was interviewed by Brazilian TV channels such as SBT Repórter (SBT TV) on August, 26th, 2009 and appeared on CQC show on September 14th, 2009 (Rede BandeirantesTV), where he expressed his ideas.He also lectured in events such as Congresso de Ufologia Trilogica de Cambuquira in 2006 and made occasional contributions to the Brazilian UFO magazine,especially issue nr.125,year XXII, "Reflexão sobre o Islamismo e os Ufos".

BIBLIOGRAPHY

Armond, Edgard-Os Exilados da Capela,Ed.Aliança,1987,1ª edição, 3ª reimpressão.

Benitez,J.J.-O Homem que Sussurrava aos Ummitas, Ed.Planeta do Brasil.

Bergier,Jacques –Os extraterrestres na História. Ed. 70,2ª Ed.,1976.

Bianca, M.A.O. –As possibilidades do infinito. Editora e Distribuidora Kopyon Ltda. 1ª Ed. 1987

Cannon,Dolores-The Custodians.Beyund Abduction-Ozark Mountain Publishing,1st edition,1999.

Campos, Pedro de- Um Vermelho Encarnado no Céu, Lúmen Editorial Ltda.,#1ª edição, 2006

Chamish,Barry -Return of the Giants, Ed.Lulu (www.lulu.com), Self Edited

Couto, Sergio Pereira –Seitas Secretas. Ed. Universo dos Livros,2007.

Daniken, Erich Von - Eram os Deuses Astronautas (Erinnerungen Von Zukunft) 1ª Ed.1968, Ed. Melhoramentos.

Fonseca, Laércio- Física Quântica e Espiritualidade. Self Edited.

Fonseca, Laércio- Câmara de Contatos, DVD Self Edited.

Granchi, Irene - Ufos e Abduções no Brasil Nove Milênio Editora, 1st edition, 1992

Hind,Cynthia-Ufos,Contatos Africanos,Livraria Francisco Alves Editora, 1987.

Icke, David - The Reptilian Agenda, DVD documentary, directed by David Icke, Ufo TV, 2004.

Jacobs, David - A ameaça Ed. Rosa dos Tempos 1ª Ed. 2002

Jacobs, David - A Vida Secreta Ed. Rosa dos tempos, 1998.

Lake, Gina - Contato Extraterrestre Ed. Pensamento, 1st edition, 1997.

Lake, Gina –The Extraterrial Vision-Channeled teachings from Theodore.Oughten House international: 2nd edition, May 1994.

Larkins,Lisette –Listening to Extraterrials ,Hampton Roads Publishing Co.,2004.

Levenda, Peter- Stairway to Heaven, Continuum Editions,2008

Levenda, Peter –Unholy Alliance, Avon Books(Mm),1995

Mack, John E –Abduction Human Encounters with Aliens, Ed. Ballantine Books 1a ed.1995.

Moura, Gilda - Ufo Contacto Alienígena, Ed. Atheneu Cultura, 1994.

Penteado, Francisco - Revista Ufo, no. 125, ano XXII Reflexões sobre o Islamismo e os Ufos. Leia também: http://www.sacred-texts.com/ufo/jinns (sobre islamismo e os ufos)

Petit, Marco Antonio- Ufos, Espiritualidade e Reencarnação Ed do Conhecimento, 1st Edition 2004

Pratt, Bob - Perigo Alienígena no Brasil - Ed. Centro Brasileiro de Pesquisas de discos Voadores-CBPDV Coleção Biblioteca Ufo.

Raimundo,José Guilherme –O Portal ,Contatos Alienígenas Ed. Madras

Rangel, Mario Nogueira-Seqüestro Alienígenas, Ed. Centro Brasileiro de Pesquisas de discos Voadores-CBPDV, 2001

Ribera, Antonio- El mistério de Ummo, Aims Intl. Books Corp; 1st Ed. (Jan. 1996)

Sitchin, Zecharia – O 12° planeta Ed. Nova Cultural 1st Edition,1999

Sparks, Jim –The Keepers, Ed. Wild Flower Press, 2006

Uchoa, A Moacyr - A Parapsicologia e os Discos Voadores Ed. Horizonte, Brasília, 1979

Uchoa, A Moacyr - Mergulho no Hiperespaço-Dimensões Esotéricas nas Pesquisas dos discos Voadores   3rd edition 1981   Ed. Horizonte, Brasília

Wells, C.R.P. -Os Semeadores da Vida- Ícone Editora, 1994

IMPORTANT SITES

Herbert Schirmer abduction:

<http://www.ufoevidence.org/cases/case659.htm>

About Pamela Stonebrooke:

<http://ufoexperiences.blogspot.com/2006/01/pamela-stonebrooke.html>

<http://www.coasttocoastam.com/show/2002/03/24>

About David Icke:

<http://www.davidicke.com> Official site

About reptilians:

<http://www.greatdreams.com/reptlan/reps.htm>

<http://en.wikipedia.org/wiki/Reptilians>,

About Rama/Sunesis group:

<http://www.sunesis.ca/>

About Bianca and Karran:

<http://www.tfca.com.br/curso_tfca.html>

About Samael Aum Weor:

<http://www.gnosisonline.org/Quem_e_Samael/index.shtml>

About Dale Russel and the Troodon

<http://www.daviddarling.info/encyclopedia/D/dinosaurint
ell.html>

http://www.cosmosmagazine.com/features/print/1444/sm
artasaurus

About Professor Laércio Fonseca:

http://www.laerciofonseca.com/

Contact the author:

chicopenteado@hotmail.com (email)